PRAXIS

A Brief Rhetoric

Carol Lea Clark

University of Texas | El Paso

FOUNTAINHEAD
PRESS

Our green initiatives include:

Electronic Products
We deliver products in non-paper form whenever possible. This includes pdf downloadables, flash drives, & CDs.

Electronic Samples
We use Xample, a new electronic sampling system. Instructor samples are sent via a personalized web page that links to pdf downloads.

FSC Certified Printers
All of our printers are certified by the Forest Service Council which promotes environmentally and socially responsible management of the world's forests. This program allows consumer groups, individual consumers, and businesses to work together hand-in-hand to promote responsible use of the world's forests as a renewable and sustainable resource.

Recycled Paper
Most of our products are printed on a minimum of 30% post-consumer waste recycled paper.

Support of Green Causes
When we do print, we donate a portion of our revenue to green causes. Listed below are a few of the organizations that have received donations from Fountainhead Press. We welcome your feedback and suggestions for contributions, as we are always searching for worthy initiatives.
Rainforest 2 Reef
Environmental Working Group

Design by Susan Moore

For information, please call or write:

1-800-586-0330
Fountainhead Press
Southlake, TX 76092

Web site: www.fountainheadpress.com
E-mail: customerservice@fountainheadpress.com

ISBN: 978-1-59871-129-5

Printed in the United States of America

Praxis

A Brief Rhetoric

The term praxis can be translated as "process" or "practice," or "experience." However, Aristotle used the term in a special way, to specify practical reasoning, for which the goal was action. *Praxis: A Brief Rhetoric* takes the rich history of rhetoric and applies it to everyday writing situations students encounter in their lives in the university, work, home, and beyond. Praxis informs students of the language of historical rhetoric, including terms such as *kairos, ethos, pathos,* and *logos.* Then, it applies this useful vocabulary to modern day issues such as airline travelers being stranded on runways, the rights of smokers and non-smokers, and global warming.

This textbook is written for instructors who have essentially the same practical goals as did Aristotle and other rhetors who taught in ancient Greece—to help their students improve their composition skills and, by doing so, increase confidence in their ability to handle any occasion for writing. To achieve these goals, instructors must focus on several distinct but interconnected skills—reading critically, researching subjects formally and informally, understanding audience expectations, utilizing the structure of language to organize and to communicate information for a specific purpose; persuading readers through appropriate use of ethos, pathos, and logos; and revising to improve effectiveness of a draft. The goal of *Praxis* is moving the student from theory to practical reason to action.

Praxis Table of Contents

CHAPTER 3   ARGUING RHETORICALLY   **54**

CHAPTER 7   REVISING RHETORICALLY   160

What is Rhetoric?

The word **rhetoric** is a good example of a word whose meaning has changed dramatically over time. You have probably heard someone say of a politician's speech, "Oh, that's just rhetoric," meaning that the politician's words are just empty verbiage or hot air. The politician was attempting to sound impressive while saying nothing that had real meaning or perhaps making promises he or she had no intention of keeping—essentially engaging in verbal deception. However, in the field of composition and writing studies, rhetoric has a much different meaning. Though definitions vary from one practitioner to another, rhetoric generally means the study and use of persuasion, a meaning that traces its roots back to the original use of the term by ancient Greeks and Romans.

During the golden age of Greece and Rome, from 500 B.C.E. to 100 C.E., art, architecture, and literature thrived. Rhetoric, in the form of oratory, was essential to both societies, as Greeks and Romans employed rhetoric to resolve disputes in the law courts and to promote political action. Philosophers such as Socrates, Plato and Aristotle, and the Roman rhetoricians Quintillian and Cicero were aware of the possible abuses of rhetoric, but to them, rhetoric was an integral part of public life, as well as the primary means of educating young people in their future roles as citizens. Philosophers in ancient Greece and Rome wrote books about rhetoric which became the basis of the teaching of writing and other essential subjects that have influenced the educational process ever since.

Aristotle defined rhetoric as "the faculty of discovering, in a given instance, the available means of persuasion," which we might paraphrase as the power to see the means of persuasion available in any given situation. Each part of this definition is important. Rhetoric is power; for the person who is able to speak eloquently, choosing the most suitable arguments about a topic for a specific audience in a particular situation, is the person most likely to persuade. In both Greece and Rome, the primary use of rhetoric was oratory, persuasion through public speaking. However, texts of many famous speeches were recorded and studied as models by students, and prominent rhetoricians wrote treatises and handbooks for teaching rhetoric. To Greeks and Romans, a person who could use rhetoric effectively was a person of influence and power because he could persuade his audience to action. The effective orator could win court cases; the effective orator could influence the passage or failure of laws; the effective orator could send a nation to war or negotiate peace.

Skill with rhetoric has conveyed power through the ages, though in our contemporary world, rhetoric is often displayed in written text such as a book, newspaper or magazine article, or scientific report, rather than as a speech. Persuasive communication can also be expressed visually, as an illustration that accompanies a text or a cartoon that conveys its own message. Indeed, in our high visual society with television, movies, video games, and the Internet, images can often persuade more powerfully than words alone.

Using rhetoric effectively means being able to interpret the rhetoric we are presented with in our everyday lives. Knowledge of persuasive communication or rhetoric empowers us to present our views and persuade others to modify their ideas. Through changes in ideas, rhetoric leads to action. Through changes in actions, rhetoric affects society.

SELECTED DEFINITIONS OF RHETORIC

Aristotle, 350 B.C.E.—*Rhetoric is "the faculty of discovering, in a given instance the available means of persuasion."*

Cicero, 90 C.E.—*Rhetoric is "speech designed to persuade." Also, "eloquence based on the rules of art."*

Quintillan, 95 C.E. —*Rhetoric is "the science of speaking well."*

Augustine of Hippo, ca. 426 C.E. —*Rhetoric is "the art of persuading people to accept something, whether it is true or false."*

Anonymous, ca. 1490–1495,—*Rhetoric is "the science which refreshes the hungry, renders the mute articulate, makes the blind see, and teaches one to avoid every lingual ineptitude."*

Heinrich Cornelius Agrippa, 1531—*"To confess the truth, it is generally granted that the entire discipline of rhetoric from start to finish is nothing other than an art of flattery, adulation, and, as some say more audaciously, lying, in that, if it cannot persuade others through the truth of the case, it does so by means of deceitful speech."*

Hoyt Hudson, 1923—*"In this sense, plainly, the man who speaks most persuasively uses the most, or certainly the best, rhetoric; and the man whom we censure for inflation of style and strained effects is suffering not from too much rhetoric, but from a lack of it."*

I. A. Richards, 1936—*"Rhetoric, I shall urge, should be a study of misunderstanding and its remedies."*

Sister Miriam Joseph, 1937—*Rhetoric is "the art of communicating thought from one mind to another, the adaptation of language to circumstance. "*

Kenneth Burke, 1950—*"[T]he basic function of rhetoric [is] the use of words by human agents to form attitudes or to induce actions in other human agents."*

Gerard A. Hauser, 2002—*"Rhetoric, as an area of study, is concerned with how humans use symbols, especially language, to reach agreement that permits coordinated effort of some sort."*

 **ACTIVITY 1.1**   **HISTORICAL USAGE OF THE WORD "RHETORIC"**

Read through the list of the historical definitions of the word "rhetoric" shown above, and choose one that you find interesting. In a discussion, compare your chosen definition with those of your classmates.

ACTIVITY
1.2   CONTEMPORARY USAGE OF THE WORD "RHETORIC"

Find at least two recent but different occasions when the word "rhetoric" is used. For example, search your local newspaper for an example of how the word "rhetoric" is being used. A search of the *Dallas Morning News* for the word "rhetoric" led to a story about citizen efforts to clean up a neglected area of town: "He now hopes for help to finally fill the gap between rhetoric and reality." Or ask a friend, fellow employee, or a family member to tell you what the word "rhetoric" means and write down what they say. Bring your examples to class and compare them to those other students in a class discussion.

WHAT IS PRAXIS?

The term **praxis** can be translated as "process" or "practice," or "experience." However, Aristotle used the term in a special way, to specify practical reasoning, for which the goal was action. Aristotle lists praxis among the three kinds of knowledge corresponding to different forms of human activities: contemplative (theoria), practical (praxis) and productive (poiesis). To be practical in the Aristotelian sense is a little different from what "being practical" means today. It indicates the ability to apply theory to concrete situations, to make things work in a complex circumstance as opposed to one who is impractical or unrealistic. However, praxis in the Aristotelian sense also has a creative element that raises it above the mundane or pragmatic.

With praxis there is no knowledge ahead of time of the right means by which we achieve a good outcome in a particular situation. In terms of rhetoric, this means that the rhetor, confronted with a speaking or writing situation, seeks the means appropriate to a particular situation. As a rhetor thinks about the purpose to be achieved, he or she invents, then perhaps revises, the persuasive means to achieve that purpose.

JET BLUE: RHETORICAL WORDS, RHETORICAL ACTIONS

For years, Jet Blue was one of the few success stories in the sometimes troubled aviation industry in the United States, offering low-cost and efficient service to a loyal clientele of often repeat customers. Then came the 2007 Valentine's Day weekend snowstorm that paralyzed the Northeast and caused cancellation or delays of hundreds of Jet Blue flights. More than 1000 passengers were stranded on nine different Jet Blue flights at John F. Kennedy International Airport alone, for "what must have seemed like an eternity," according to the *New York Times*. A plane to Aruba full of passengers was delayed on the tarmac for a reported 11 hours. Even before the crisis was resolved, passengers and airline critics began what people do in times of crisis—engage in rhetoric or persuasive communication. Newspaper editorials and Blog articles called the airline "unprepared" and the situation a "debacle." Spokespersons from a variety of consumer groups appeared on radio and television talk shows, calling for congressional action to establish a "bill of rights" for airline passengers. Some industry watchers predicted permanent damage to Jet Blue's image.

The airline, however, responded quickly to this crisis situation with rhetorical actions designed to minimize the damage. CEO David Neeleman apologized in a press conference: "We're sorry. We're humiliated. This isn't like us. This isn't the Jet Blue you've known for the last seven years. This is what we're doing to make sure it doesn't happen again." The "this" Neeleman was referring to was a "Jet Blue Airways' Customer Bill of Rights," to be applied retroactively, with passengers stranded during the Valentine's Day weekend receiving compensation depending on the degree of inconvenience.

In addition, the airline also took action that avoided a repetition of the problem. Less than two weeks after the Valentine's Day delays, Jet Blue was one of five airlines that together cancelled over 1000 flights due to another ice storm. By canceling flights rather than boarding passengers on flights that might wait on the taxi ways for hours before takeoff, Jet Blue and the other airlines avoided the chance any of the airlines would repeat the Valentine's Day crisis. While Jet Blue and the other airlines took some heat from inconvenienced passengers for canceling flights, Jet Blue was no longer being singled out as a flawed performer in the airline industry.

What was rhetorical about the company's words and actions? If we take our paraphrase of Aristotle as our definition of rhetoric—the power to see the means of persuasion available in any given situation—the company identified an honest apology combined with compensation for affected passengers as one means to persuade customers of their willingness to take responsibility for the inconvenience and distress passengers experienced Valentine's weekend in 2007. Also, by issuing a Customer Bill of Rights they diffused efforts by activist groups to lobby for a law specifying passenger rights, an outcome the airline industry wanted to avoid. Then, the company's action of canceling flights during the next major snowstorm rather than stranding passengers on airplanes demonstrated their commitment not to repeat the Valentine's Day errors. Jet Blue's actions also involved praxis, for they were practical efforts to repair the company's reputation, and they were actions that had to be developed as events unfolded in an unprecedented situation.

Although the company words and actions were described by some editorials as "too little, too late," the company apparently achieved its purpose of restoring consumer confidence, subject to future events. If Jet Blue experiences another crisis down the road, however, the memory of the February 2007 crisis might resurface, and the airline would have to take additional and perhaps more extreme measures to restore its image.

JetBlue Airways' Customer Bill of Rights

Above all else, JetBlue Airways is dedicated to bringing humanity back to air travel. We strive to make every part of your experience as simple and as pleasant as possible. Unfortunately, there are times when things do not go as planned. If you're inconvenienced as a result, we think it is important that you know exactly what you can expect from us. That's why we created our Customer Bill of Rights. These Rights will always be subject to the highest level of safety and security for our customers and crewmembers.

INFORMATION

JetBlue will notify customers of the following:

* Delays prior to scheduled departure
* Cancellations and their cause
* Diversions and their cause

CANCELLATIONS

All customers whose flight is cancelled by JetBlue will, at the customer's option, receive a full refund or reaccommodation on the next available JetBlue flight at no additional charge or fare. If JetBlue cancels a flight within 4 hours of scheduled departure and the cancellation is due to a *Controllable Irregularity*, JetBlue will also issue the customer a $100 Voucher good for future travel on JetBlue.

DELAYS [Departure Delays or Onboard Ground Delays on Departure]

For customers whose flight is delayed 3 hours or more after scheduled departure, JetBlue will provide free movies on flights that are 2 hours or longer.

DEPARTURE DELAYS

1. Customers whose flight is delayed for 1-1:59 hours after scheduled departure time due to a *Controllable Irregularity* are entitled to a $25 Voucher good for future travel on JetBlue.
2. Customers whose flight is delayed for 2-3:59 hours after scheduled departure time due to a *Controllable Irregularity* are entitled to a $50 Voucher good for future travel on JetBlue.
3. Customers whose flight is delayed for 4-5:59 hours after scheduled departure time due to a *Controllable Irregularity* are entitled to a Voucher good for future travel on JetBlue in the amount paid by the customer for the oneway trip.
4. Customers whose flight is delayed for 6 or more hours after scheduled departure time due to a *Controllable Irregularity* are entitled to a Voucher good for future travel on JetBlue in the amount paid by the customer for the roundtrip (or the oneway trip, doubled).

ONBOARD GROUND DELAYS

JetBlue will provide customers experiencing an Onboard Ground Delay with 36 channels of DIRECTV°* food and drink, access to clean restrooms and, as necessary, medical treatment. For customers who experience an Onboard Ground Delay for more than 5 hours, JetBlue will also take necessary action so that customers may deplane.

Arrivals:

1. Customers who experience an Onboard Ground Delay on Arrival for 1-1:59 hours after scheduled arrival time are entitled to a $50 Voucher good for future travel on JetBlue.
2. Customers who experience an Onboard Ground Delay on Arrival for 2 hours or more after scheduled arrival time are entitled to a Voucher good for future travel on JetBlue in the amount paid by the customer for the roundtrip (or the oneway trip, doubled).

Departures:

1. Customers who experience an Onboard Ground Delay on Departure after scheduled departure time for 3-3:59 hours are entitled to a $50 Voucher good for future travel on JetBlue.
2. Customers who experience an Onboard Ground Delay on Departure after scheduled departure time for 4 or more hours are entitled to a Voucher good for future travel on JetBlue in the amount paid by the customer for the roundtrip (or the oneway trip, doubled).

In-flight entertainment:

JetBlue offers 36 channels of DIRECTV° service on its flights in the Continental U.S. If our LiveTV™ system is inoperable on flights in the Continental U.S., or if we cannot offer free movies on flights outside the Continental U.S. that are 2 hours or longer, JetBlue will issue the customer a $15 Voucher good for future travel on JetBlue.

OVERBOOKINGS (As defined in JetBlue's Contract of Carriage)

Customers who are involuntarily denied boarding shall receive $1,000.

JetBlue Airways
118-29 Queens Blvd
Forest Hills, NY 11375

LAST UPDATED: 10/2007

These Rights are subject to JetBlue's Contract of Carriage and, as applicable, the operational control of the flight crew, and apply to only JetBlue-operated flights. *Available only on flights in the Continental U.S.

This document is representative of what is reflected in JetBlue's Contract of Carriage, the legally binding document between JetBlue and its customers.

ACTIVITY 1.3   EVALUATE JET BLUE'S RHETORICAL ACTIONS

Re-read the Jet Blue Airways' Customer Bill of Rights and, in a group, discuss the following questions:

1. What commitment does Jet Blue make about notifications to passengers?
2. What specifications does Jet Blue make about conditions on aircraft for flights experiencing an on-board ground delay?
3. Do the financial compensations Jet Blue outlines for delayed or cancelled flights seem appropriate and fair? Why or why not?
4. Why does Jet Blue say that they are issuing a Customer Bill of Rights?
5. Now that you have examined the Customer Bill of Rights in detail, what impression does it persuade you to have about the airline?
6. On a scale of 1 to 10, what rating would you give Jet Blue in terms of their use of praxis or practical reasoning during this crisis? Why?

ACTIVITY 1.4   EXAMINE BUSINESS RHETORIC

As a group examine the rhetoric of a corporation, business or service. Consult the company's website, make a site visit, evaluate advertising, press releases, or other texts, or otherwise collect texts that the company issues to promote its image. Discuss what the company is trying to tell clients or consumers through their public texts and visuals. Evaluate whether they are successful in projecting the image you think they want to project.

MEMORIES OF MCDONALD'S RHETORICAL ACTION 20 YEARS LATER

In 1984, a disgruntled unemployed security guard, James Oliver Huberty, shot and killed 21 people, including five children and six teenagers, in a McDonald's in San Ysidro, California, as well as wounding 19 others. The gunman's rampage lasted 77 minutes before he was shot and killed by a police sniper, and it was the worst shooting incident in the United States to that date. People throughout the United States were universally outraged. Afterwards, police forces revised their procedures for dealing with mass shootings, in particular the formation of SWAT units and mental health response teams.

Shortly after the shooting, a committee in San Ysidro collected 1,400 signatures asking that the McDonald's be razed and a memorial park built. Although McDonald's was in no way responsible for the attack, they responded to the committee's rhetorical appeal. Bob Kaiser, director of media relations for McDonald's, said, "The concern is for the people, not simply business" and reported that the company's decision whether to reopen the restaurant was being held in abeyance. Later, the company tore down the restaurant and donated the land to the city. After debating what to do with the land, the city used it to build a community college.

In 2004, twenty years after the massacre, a memorial service was held at the site, and the media ran stories about the anniversary. Many people contributed to a blog associated with the anniversary story in the local newspaper:

> Jennifer wrote:"I live in La Jolla, exactly twenty five miles north of the former McDonald's where this tragedy took place some twenty plus years ago. The site is now the home of Southwestern College, but I have seen the memorial and am always filled with sadness when I go there. They have done a wonderful job on the memorial which is just in front of the former McDonald's building which you can tell was once the eatery, but has been painted grey, though the general shape of the building is still there. I am especially touched by the comments in this story and it is great that the memory of what happened not so long ago in our city is kept alive. ALL those that survived or not on that very sad day, were heroes, but their memories will never be in vain and we, as the citizens of this beautiful city will always be proud of their bravery and courage."

Leonor wrote:" I was seven at the time and I lived half a block from McDonald's. I saw bullets flying in the air and I remember police officers not letting us go to our house. They told us to get down in our car and not move. It was scary because we did not know what was going on. We were going to eat at McDonald's but my grandma invited us to her house. I still live in San Ysidro and I graduated from Southwestern College and I see the area everyday. It's not easy to forget what I do remember."

Armida wrote:"I remember that day. I was there I had just turned 17. This was my first job. I lost my cousin and two friends because they threw a coffee pot at him to save this guy who became a cop. I saved a co-worker. I never told anybody or wrote about this day till now."

Sergio wrote:"I still remember this event. I'm now 33 years old and I was 9 years old. I still remember the gun shots, many of them. I grew up about 3 blocks away. I remember the countless police officers blocking the streets of Sunset Lane, which was my street. Two of my friends were murdered. I could have been there. My best friend died that day. This has been a funeral I will always remember. I just like to share a tiny bit on that day in the summer of July."

Joe Bloggs wrote: "I remember this happening. I was only about 12 years old at the time and living in Australia, but it is something I never forget about. Why America is so obsessed with guns I will never understand. Nobody except the police and army should have access to firearms. The private ownership of guns should be illegal and there should be gun amnesty' days where guns can be handed in to be crushed. This is going to happen time and time people unless you stand up and say no to gun ownership."

The blog entries show the impact of the event, even twenty years later. Notice that there are no negative comments about the McDonald's, nor about what the community decided to do with the land. Nothing McDonald's could have done would have erased the pain of the event, but their rhetorical actions, both word and action, did not add to the trauma of the event. If anything, McDonald's action in responding to the citizens' request to tear down the building and donate the land to the city is praised 20 years later.

ACTIVITY
1.5
BLOGGING AND RESPONDING TO BLOGGING

1. In your group, discuss the blog entries above about the San Ysidro shooting. Which one attracts your attention the most? What do you think was the rhetorical purpose of the entry's author?
2. Write your own text that could be submitted to a blog about the McDonald's story. What would you say to the citizens who remember the event? What would you say to the people at McDonald's who made the decision to tear down the building and donate the land to the city?
3. Do you blog? Why? Do you check frequently to see if there are responses to your comments? How do you feel if there are? How do you feel if there are not? Does it matter if the response is positive or negative?

RHETORICAL ARGUMENT

Often, in our culture, the word argument is taken to mean disagreements or even fights, with raised voices, rash words, and hurt feelings. We have the perception of an argument as something that has victory and defeat, winners and losers. Argument, in the sense of a **rhetorical argument,** however, means the carefully crafted presentation of a viewpoint or position on a topic, the giving of thoughts, ideas and opinions along with reasons for their support. The persuasive strength of the argument rests upon the rhetorical skills of the rhetor (the speaker or the writer) in utilizing the tools of language to persuade a particular audience.

Often, an argument is a dialogue—one person or group presenting one viewpoint and hearing another viewpoint in response. After the Jet Blue flight delays, citizen groups lobbied for government intervention and the establishment of a passenger bill of rights. Jet Blue responded by voluntarily issuing such a bill of rights. After the San Ysidro McDonald's shooting, a citizen group requested that the building be razed, and McDonald's responded by tearing down the building and donating the land to the city. Such rational arguments may occur in conversation, public speaking, or non-fiction prose.

However, contentious issues often are not so easily settled, even temporarily. For example, in the United States there is a spreading ban on smoking in restaurants, hospitals, and other public buildings because of evidence that even second hand smoke can cause health problems. Many smokers, though, think that forbidding smoking in public, including parking lots and other outdoor spaces, is going too far. A recent opinion piece in a Florida newspaper responding to a hospital's ban on smoking in the parking lot says,

> I respect my fellow citizens and their wish to breathe clean air and have always kept my distance from others when I am smoking, out of common courtesy. However, recent policies banning cigarette smoking based on political correctness or personal bias and certainly not law are becoming far beyond reasonable....[It is] ridiculous because if these hospital administrators were so concerned about the quality of the air on their "campuses," they would also ban motor vehicles on their premises. But no, those very administrators who target the few remaining cigarette smokers are probably driving to work in their SUVs and polluting the air far more than a stressed-out patient or visitor who smokes.

In contrast, a Massachusetts beach town banned smoking at its public beaches because of complaints about second hand smoke and cigarette butts littering the beaches. The chairman of the town's Recreation Commission, according to an article in the *Boston Globe*, said, "There were a number [of complaints] about little children playing in the beach, and next thing you know, they come back and have cigarette butts in their hands. There were a few comments about smoke and smelling, but mainly it was the disposal." A local pulmonary physician, according to the article, commented in a letter to the commission, "People seemed truly astonished that playing ball was prohibited [at the beach] but smoking within a few feet of young children or even pregnant women was permissible."

What do you think? Do smokers have rights that are violated by bans on smoking in public places? Read the following controversial essay by Stanley S. Scott, "Smokers Get a Raw Deal" and think about your reaction to the argument he presents.

**READING
1.1**

"SMOKERS GET A RAW DEAL"

Originally printed as an Op-Ed in the New York Times, Stanley Scott's essay continues to be controversial because it portrays smokers as the victims of discrimination. One letter to the editor in response to Scott's essay said that Scott "debases the concept of civil rights in his plea for the 'basic freedoms" of American smokers." At the time he wrote the essay, Scott was a vice president and director of corporate affairs at Phillip Morris Inc., a tobacco company.

Copyright 1984 The New York Times   —*NEW YORK SATURDAY, DECEMBER 29, 1984*—

Smokers Get a Raw Deal

By Stanley S. Scott

The civil rights act, the voting rights act and a host of antidiscrimination laws notwithstanding, millions of Americans are still forced to sit in the back of planes, trains and buses. Many more are subject to segregation in public places. Some are even denied housing and employment: victims of an alarming—yet socially acceptable—public hostility.

This new form of discrimination is based on smoking behavior.

If you happen to enjoy a cigarette, you are the potential target of violent anti-smokers and overzealous public enforcers determined to force their beliefs on the rest of society.

Ever since people began smoking, smokers and nonsmokers have been able to live with one another using common courtesy and common sense. Not anymore. Today, smokers must put up with virtually unenforceable laws regulating when and where they can smoke—laws intended as much to discourage smoking itself as to protect the rights of nonsmokers. Much worse, supposedly responsible organizations devoted to the "public interest" are encouraging the harassment of those who smoke.

Stanley S. Scott is vice president and director of corporate affairs of Philip Morris Inc.

This year, for example, the American Cancer Society is promoting programs that encourage people to attack smokers with canisters of gas, to blast them with horns, to squirt them with oversized water guns and burn them in effigy.

Harmless fun? Not quite. Consider the incidents that are appearing on police blotters across America:

• In a New York restaurant, a young man celebrating with friends was zapped in the face by a man with the aerosol spray can. His offense: lighting a cigarette. The aggressor was the head of a militant anti-smoker organization whose goal is to mobilize an army of two million zealots to spray

Zealots, stop maltreating cigarette users

• In a suburban Seattle drug store, a man puffing on a cigarette while he waited for a prescription to be filled was ordered to stop by an elderly customer who pulled a gun on him.

• A 23-year-old lit up a cigarette on a Los Angeles bus. A passenger objected. When the smoker objected to the objection, he was fatally stabbed.

• A transit policeman, using his reserve gun, shot and fatally wounded a man on a subway train in the Bronx in a shootout over smoking cigarettes.

The basic freedoms of more than 50 million American smokers are at risk today. Tomorrow, who knows what personal behavior will become socially unacceptable, subject to restrictive laws and public ridicule? Could travel by private car make the social engineers' hit list because it is less safe than public transit? Could ice cream, cake and cookies become socially unacceptable because their consumption causes obesity? What about sky diving, mountain climbing, skiing and contact sports? How far will we allow this to spread?

The question all Americans must ask themselves is: can a nation that has struggled so valiantly to eliminate bias based on race, religion and sex afford to allow a fresh set of categories to encourage new forms of hostility between large groups of citizens?

After all, discrimination is discrimination, no matter what it is based on.

ACTIVITY 1.6

DISCUSS "SMOKERS GET A RAW DEAL"

In your group discuss the following questions about Scott's essay:
- Does he make a strong case for his position that smokers are the victims of discrimination? Why or why not?
- Scott does not refer to the counter argument that people are harmed by second hand smoke. How does that affect the credibility of his argument?
- Since Scott's essay, "Smokers Get a Raw Deal" was written, the places where smokers can legally have a cigarette has dwindled markedly. If Scott were writing his essay today, how do you think that would change his argument?

ENCOUNTERING VISUAL RHETORIC

This is an example of one of the "I'm a Mac" Macintosh advertisements. This one portrays the PC as bloated and awkward.

Contemporary America is a highly visual culture with television, the Internet, and video games. Even in a more static form, print advertisements, such as the Apple "I'm a Mac" ad above, can be highly persuasive, especially when combined with a parallel television campaign based on the same theme, as Apple has done with these ads. CNet News, part of the CNet website that reviews new computerized products, reported that a CoreBrands study showed that Microsoft's brand ranked number 59 in 2007, down from 11 in 2004. They raised the question of whether the "I'm a Mac" ads that portray a PC as an outdated, bumbling, middle-aged character and Mac as a cool, with-it young man might be partially responsible. Following the "I'm a Mac" ads, Microsoft launched its own "I'm a PC" line of advertisements designed to counter the negative images of Microsoft's software portrayed in the Apple ad campaign.

Why is a visual so powerful? Colors, shapes, and symbols impact a viewer in ways text alone cannot. An image can instantly present an argument, and because it is visual, it communicates more quickly and, sometimes, more powerfully than do words. When a visual image is combined with a very few well chosen words, its ability to persuade can be significant, as anyone would know whose child, after watching the ads shown during Saturday cartoons, insists upon buying Captain Crunch or Coco Puffs cereal.

**ACTIVITY
1.7**   **COMMUNICATIVE POWER OF ADVERTISEMENTS**

Find a print advertisement in a magazine you read frequently and bring the ad to class. In your small group, discuss what is the persuasive message of each advertisement and whether the ad does an effective job of persuading its audience of magazine readers.

For example, if you were in the market for a personal computer, would the "I'm a Mac" advertisement above have an influence on your decision of what computer to purchase? You might consider whether you identify with the images portrayed in the advertisement. Are you a "Mac person" or a "PC person"? Or do you see yourself differently as a computer person? Also, are there other factors involved in your purchase decision such as cost and availability of software?

With each of the advertisements your group brings to class, consider whether you react to the advertisement the way you imagine the company wants you to react. Evaluate the likelihood that you would purchase the product depicted in the advertisement, should you be in the market for that type of product. In other words, you may think that an ad is really funny, clever, or beautiful, but that does not necessarily mean that the company has "sold" you on its product. Some advertisements work better than others, and you, as a consumer, can evaluate their effectiveness.

WHY STUDY RHETORIC?

Rhetoric, or persuasive communication, happens all around us every day, in conversation at the grocery store, in blogs, on television, and in the classroom. We Americans constantly air our opinions about almost everything. Sometimes it is to convince others to share our opinions, sometimes the reason is to engage in a dialog that will help us understand the world around us, and sometimes it is to persuade others to action. Argument is essential to human interaction and to society, for it is through the interplay of ideas in argument that we discover answers to problems, try out new ideas, shape scientific experiments, communicate with family members, recruit others to join a team, and work out any of the multitude of human interactions essential for society to function.   When issues are complex, arguments do not result in immediate persuasion of the audience; rather, argument is part of an on-going conversation between concerned parties who seek resolution, rather than speedy answers.

Rhetoric provides a useful framework for looking at the world, as well as for evaluating and initiating communications. In the modern world, writing and communicating persuasively is a necessary skill. Those who can present effective arguments in writing are, in the business world, often the ones who are promoted. In addition, those who are able to evaluate the arguments presented to them, whether by politicians, advertisers, or even family members, are less likely to be swayed by logical fallacies or ill supported research.

Also, writing rhetorically is a tool with sometimes surprising uses. Research shows that, as students, we are more likely to remember material we have written about rather than simply memorized. Also, writers often find that they initiate ideas and connections between ideas when they write that they might not otherwise have found, thus writing to discover.

Being able to use the tools of rhetoric effectively gives the user power to control his or her communication—both incoming and outgoing—in everyday use.

**ACTIVITY
1.8**

WRITING ABOUT EVERYDAY ARGUMENTS

Read your local newspaper, and news magazines such as *Time* or *Newsweek*, or search the Internet and bring to class a copy of a recent text or visual image that makes an argument about an issue. You might find, for example, an editorial in your local newspaper about recycling efforts in your community or a blog entry about parenting practices. Be sure, however, that the text or image takes a position on the issue. Write a paragraph of approximately 100 to 150 words describing the argument to your classmates and your reaction to it.

THINKING CRITICALLY, READING RHETORICALLY

A major focus of studying texts in contemporary times is upon encouraging students to develop critical thinking, a skill which is essential for understanding the scientific method and for making effective judgments in the workplace and in civil life. This student-centered emphasis would have seemed strange to ancient Greek and Roman rhetoricians and their students. They believed that a rhetor's skill was best developed by honoring the skills of those who have excelled in the past. Therefore, a large part of the educational process involved having students study texts of well-regarded speeches, memorizing and reciting them, and modeling new compositions on their approaches to topics and language style. Isocrates explained:

> Since language is of such a nature that it is possible to discourse on the same subject matter in many different ways—to represent the great as lowly or invest the little with grandeur, to recount the things of old in a new manner or set forth events of recent date in an old fashion—it follows that one must not shun the subjects upon which others have composed before, but must try to compose better than they... (Panegyricus).

Thus, students in ancient Greece or Rome would have been presented with a text, often read aloud by a teacher, and they would be asked to transcribe or copy it down with the idea that they would internalize the skills of the master rhetor who had originally given the speech. Then, they would be asked to write about the same subject in a way that built upon what they had learned from the master text but incorporated their own personal attitudes or perspectives.

Today, rather than being asked to model new compositions upon the techniques of classic texts, students are asked to read texts carefully and then to engage in critical thinking and discussion about those texts.

To think critically is to think both reflectively and independently. Critical thinkers do not believe facts or opinions just because they are published—whether it is in newspapers, textbooks, on television, or on the Internet. Nor do they focus upon just understanding or memorizing information, as in facts and figures. Critical thinkers examine the reasoning of the information in front of them, looking for premises, and considering the inferences drawn from those premises. They are able to think for themselves, making logical connections between ideas, seeing cause and effect relationships, and using information to solve problems. **Reading rhetorically**, whether you call it that or not, is an important component of critical thinking because it involves evaluating texts for validity of arguments, adequacy of evidence, and presence of bias.

APPLY CRITICAL READING TO A SPEECH

On November 4, 2008, in Grant Park, Chicago, Illinois, President-Elect Barack Obama presented his victory speech after winning the presidency in a contest against Republican John McCain. President-Elect Obama never mentions in his speech that he is the nation's first African-American president. He does not have to. He begins by saying, "If there is anyone out there who still doubts that America is a place where all things are possible; who still wonders if the dream of our founders is alive in our time; who still questions the power of our democracy, tonight is your answer." Simply standing before the crowd, he visually illustrates his own point—an African-American can become president in America.

To begin an analysis of the victory speech, you might want to watch the speech, even if you have seen it before. One place you can find it on the Internet is at the American Rhetoric site, http://www.americanrhetoric. com. As you listen to the speech, think about how Obama has crafted his text to respond to his audience of thousands in Chicago and millions around the world. For example, he begins by saying, "Hello, Chicago," acknowledging those immediately before him. Then later, he addresses his larger audience, "And to all those watching tonight from beyond our shores, from parliaments and palaces, to those who are huddled around radios in the forgotten corners of the world, our stories are singular, but our destiny is shared, and a new dawn of American leadership is at hand." As you read (or listen), be aware of what the president-elect has to say to his different audiences. What are his premises, and what inferences does he make from those premises?

READING
2.1

"PRESIDENT-ELECT VICTORY SPEECH"

November 4, 2008

Hello, Chicago.

If there is anyone out there who still doubts that America is a place where all things are possible; who still wonders if the dream of our founders is alive in our time; who still questions the power of our democracy, tonight is your answer.

It's the answer told by lines that stretched around schools and churches in numbers this nation has never seen; by people who waited three hours and four hours, many for the very first time in their lives, because they believed that this time must be different; that their voices could be that difference.

It's the answer spoken by young and old, rich and poor, Democrat and Republican, black, white, Hispanic, Asian, Native American, gay, straight, disabled and not disabled—Americans who sent a message to the world that we have never been just a collection of individuals or a collection of Red States and Blue States: we are, and always will be, the United States of America!

It's the answer that—that led those who have been told for so long by so many to be cynical, and fearful, and doubtful about what we can achieve to put their hands on the arc of history and bend it once more toward the hope of a better day.

It's been a long time coming, but tonight, because of what we did on this day, in this election, at this defining moment, change has come to America.

A little bit earlier this evening, I received an extraordinarily gracious call from Senator McCain. Senator McCain fought long and hard in this campaign, and he's fought even longer and harder for the country that he loves. He has endured sacrifices for America that most of us cannot begin to imagine. We are better off for the service rendered by this brave and selfless leader. I congratulate him; I congratulate Governor Palin for all that they've achieved, and I look forward to working with them to renew this nation's promise in the months ahead.

I want to thank my partner in this journey, a man who campaigned from his heart and spoke for the men and women he grew up with on the streets of Scranton and rode with on the train home to Delaware, the Vice President-Elect of the United States, Joe Biden.

And I would not be standing here tonight without the unyielding support of my best friend for the last 16 years, the rock of our family, the love of my life, the nation's next First Lady: Michelle Obama.

Sasha and Malia, I love you both more than you can imagine, and you have earned the new puppy that's coming with us to the White House. And while she's no longer with us, I know my grandmother's watching, along with the family that made me who I am. I miss them tonight, and I know that my debt to them is beyond measure. To my sister Maya, my sister Alma, all my other brothers and sisters—thank you so much for the support that you've given me. I am grateful to them.

And to my campaign manager, David Plouffe—the unsung hero of this campaign, who built the best—the best political campaign, I think, in the history of the United States of America. To my chief strategist David Axelrod—who's been a partner with me every step of the way. To the best campaign team ever assembled in the history of politics—you made this happen, and I am forever grateful for what you've sacrificed to get it done.

But above all, I will never forget who this victory truly belongs to. It belongs to you. It belongs to you. I was never the likeliest candidate for this office. We didn't start with much money or many endorsements. Our campaign was not hatched in the halls of Washington. It began in the backyards of Des Moines and the living rooms of Concord and the front porches of Charleston. It was built by working men and women who dug into what little savings they had to give 5 dollars and 10 dollars and 20 dollars to the cause. It grew strength from the young people who rejected the myth of their generation's apathy, who left their homes and their families for jobs that offered little pay and less sleep. It drew strength from the not-so-young people who braved the bitter cold and scorching heat to knock on doors of perfect strangers, and from the millions of Americans who volunteered and organized and proved that more than two centuries later a government of the people, by the people, and for the people has not perished from the Earth. This is your victory.

And I know you didn't do this just to win an election. And I know you didn't do it for me. You did it because you understand the enormity of the task that lies ahead. For even as we celebrate tonight, we know the challenges that tomorrow will bring are the greatest of our lifetime: two wars, a planet in peril, the worst financial crisis in a century. Even as we stand here tonight, we know there are brave Americans waking up in the deserts of Iraq and the mountains of Afghanistan to risk their lives for us. There are mothers and fathers who will lie awake after the children fall asleep and wonder how they'll make the mortgage or pay their doctors' bills or save enough for their child's college education. There's new energy to harness, new jobs to be created, new schools to build, and threats to meet, alliances to repair.

The road ahead will be long. Our climb will be steep. We may not get there in one year or even in one term. But, America, I have never been more hopeful than I am tonight that we will get there. I promise you, we as a people will get there.

There will be setbacks and false starts. There are many who won't agree with every decision or policy I make as President. And we know the government can't solve every problem. But I will always be honest with you about the challenges we face. I will listen to you, especially when we disagree. And, above all, I will ask you to join in the work of remaking this nation, the only way it's been done in America for 221 years—block by block, brick by brick, calloused hand by calloused hand. What began 21 months ago in the depths of winter cannot end on this autumn night.

This victory alone is not the change we seek. It is only the chance for us to make that change. And that cannot happen if we go back to the way things were. It can't happen without you, without a new spirit of service, a new spirit of sacrifice. So let us summon a new spirit of patriotism, of responsibility, where each of us resolves to pitch in and work harder and look after not only ourselves but each other. Let us remember that, if this financial crisis taught us anything, it's that we cannot have a thriving Wall Street while Main Street suffers. In this country, we rise or fall as one nation, as one people. Let's resist the temptation to fall back on the same partisanship and pettiness and immaturity that has poisoned our politics for so long.

Let's remember that it was a man from this state who first carried the banner of the Republican Party to the White House, a Party founded on the values of self-reliance and individual liberty and national unity. Those are values that we all share. And while the Democratic Party has won a great victory tonight, we do so with a measure of humility and determination to heal the divides that have held back our progress. As Lincoln said to a nation far more divided than ours: "We are not enemies but friends...." "Though passion may have strained, it must not break our bonds of affection."

And to those Americans who—whose support I have yet to earn, I may not have won your vote tonight, but I hear your voices. I need your help. And I will be your President, too.

And to all those watching tonight from beyond our shores, from parliaments and palaces, to those who are huddled around radios in the forgotten corners of the world, our stories are singular, but our destiny is shared, and a new dawn of American leadership is at hand.

To those—To those who would tear the world down: We will defeat you. To those who seek peace and security: We support you. And to all those who have wondered if America's beacon still burns as bright: Tonight we've proved once more that the true strength of our nation comes not from the might of our arms or the scale of our wealth, but from the enduring power of our ideals: democracy, liberty, opportunity, and unyielding hope.

That's the true genius of America: that America can change. Our union can be perfected. What we've already achieved gives us hope for what we can and must achieve tomorrow.

This election had many firsts and many stories that will be told for generations. But one that's on my mind tonight's about a woman who cast her ballot in Atlanta. She's a lot like the millions of others who stood in line to make their voice heard in this election except for one thing: Ann Nixon Cooper is 106 years old.

She was born just a generation past slavery; a time when there were no cars on the road or planes in the sky; when someone like her couldn't vote for two reasons: because she was a woman and because of the color of her skin.

And tonight, I think about all that she's seen throughout her century in America—the heartache and the hope; the struggle and the progress; the times we were told that we can't, and the people who pressed on with that American creed: Yes we can.

At a time when women's voices were silenced and their hopes dismissed, she lived to see them stand up and speak out and reach for the ballot: Yes we can.

When there was despair in the dust bowl and depression across the land, she saw a nation conquer fear itself with a New Deal, new jobs, a new sense of common purpose: Yes we can.

When the bombs fell on our harbor and tyranny threatened the world, she was there to witness a generation rise to greatness and a democracy was saved: Yes we can.

She was there for the buses in Montgomery, the hoses in Birmingham, a bridge in Selma, and a preacher from Atlanta who told a people that "we shall overcome": Yes we can.

A man touched down on the moon, a wall came down in Berlin, a world was connected by our own science and imagination.

And this year, in this election, she touched her finger to a screen, and cast her vote, because after 106 years in America, through the best of times and the darkest of hours, she knows how America can change: Yes we can.

America, we have come so far. We have seen so much. But there is so much more to do. So tonight, let us ask ourselves—if our children should live to see the next century; if my daughters should be so lucky to live as long as Ann Nixon Cooper, what change will they see? What progress will we have made?

This is our chance to answer that call. This is our moment. This is our time, to put our people back to work and open doors of opportunity for our kids; to restore prosperity and promote the cause of peace; to reclaim the American dream and reaffirm that fundamental truth, that, out of many, we are one; that while we breathe, we hope. And where we are met with cynicism and doubt and those who tell us that we can't, we will respond with that timeless creed that sums up the spirit of a people: Yes, we can.

Thank you.

God bless you.

And may God bless the United States of America.

ANN NIXON COOPER

106 years old, suddenly became famous when President-Elect Barack Obama used her life as an extended analogy of how America has changed in the last 100 years. She was born in Shelbyville, Tennessee on January 9, 1902, a time before women and African Americans could vote. She has lived to see presidents come and go. In 2008 she used a touch-screen voting machine to cast her vote for the nation's first African-American president.

"I ain't got time to die," Ann Nixon Cooper, 106 years old, said with a smile. "Even if he didn't win, I was happy for him just to be nominated," said Ann Nixon Cooper. "The first black president—isn't that something, at 106 years old?"

ANALYZE AN EXTENDED ANALOGY

In President-Elect Barack Obama's victory speech, he uses the life of 106 year old Ann Nixon Cooper as an **extended analogy** to illustrate the challenges and changes in America in the last 100 years. According to Obama, Cooper experienced these events:

- She was born "a generation past slavery; a time when there were no cars on the road or planes in the sky."
- She couldn't vote for two reasons—"because she was a woman and because of the color of her skin."
- She lived through the dust bowl of the depression and the New Deal, Pearl Harbor and the winning of World War II.
- She was there for the Civil Rights Movement and "the preacher from Atlanta [Dr. Martin Luther King, Jr.] who told a people that 'we shall overcome.'"
- She watched a man touch down on the moon, a wall come down in Berlin, and the development of the Internet.
- She voted to elect Obama by "touch[ing] her finger to a screen."

All these things, of course, millions of Americans experienced along with Cooper, and, by using her example, Obama reminded his audience of Americans that they, or their parents, or their friends, had been there, too. He used her example to say, "America, we have come so far. We have seen so much. But there is so much more to do. So tonight, let us ask ourselves—if our children should live to see the next century; if my daughters should be so lucky to live as long as Ann Nixon Cooper, what change will they see? What progress will we have made?"

As an activity, discuss Obama's use of Ann Nixon Cooper as an extended analogy. Did his story of her life remind you of your life, that of your parents, or others you have known? What did you think and feel as you heard her story?

WAYS OF READING RHETORICALLY

According to reading theorist Louise Rosenblatt, when we read a text, we take the pattern of verbal signs left by the author and use them to recreate the text, not in the exact way the author perceived the text, but guided by it.

So, as we read, there is a constant stream of response to the text. However, Rosenblatt says that even as the reader is recreating the text, he or she is also reacting to it. Thus, there are two interacting streams of response involved as the person moves through the text. The reader, rather than being a passive receptor for the author's text, actually participates in the creative process during reading.

However, we read differently depending on the text and the occasion. For example, if you take a paperback novel on an airplane trip, you probably read simply for entertainment and to pass the time in the air. If you read *King Lear* for a literature class, you read for the plot, characterization, and other elements that you know will be discussed in class. If you read a chapter in your chemistry textbook before an exam, you are focusing on remembering concepts and details that might be on the test. Reading as a writer is another type of reading. You examine the text with an eye for the choices the writer made when crafting the text, such as whether the writer begins with a narrative introduction, a quote from a noted authority, or a startling statement. You notice, for example, what people are mentioned in the text, either as authorities or participants in activities.

Rosenblatt also makes a useful distinction between two main kinds of reading—aesthetic reading and efferent reading. In **aesthetic reading**, the reader is most interested in what happens "during the reading event, as he fixes his attention on the actual experience he is living through," according to Rosenblatt. Readers focus upon the ideas, images, and story of the text that evoke an aesthetic experience in the moment of reading. **Efferent readers**, in contrast, read to learn from the text, and, thus, according to Rosenblatt, "concentrate on the information, the concepts, the guides to action, that will be left with him when the reading is over."

Reading rhetorically is efferent reading, focusing not on the experience of reading but on the information the text conveys and upon the way an argument is established and supported in a text. Sometimes arguments are written in an engaging style that is a pleasure to read or sometimes in a highly emotional tone that arouses a visceral response in the reader. A text that inspires aesthetic reading must sometimes be read several times in order for the reader to focus on the structure of the argument beneath the creative language.

Some theorists say that critical thinking is "thinking about thinking" or "reasoning about reasoning," and that is exactly what reading rhetorically involves—reasoning about whether or not a text presents a reasoned argument. A good way to begin reading rhetorically is be aware of the essential elements of an argument and identify these elements in the text you are evaluating. These elements are as follows:

- A debatable issue. By definition, for a text to be an argument, there must be at least two sides that can be asserted and supported.
- A clearly stated position, claim statement, or **thesis.** Arguments assert different kinds of claims, such as taking a position on an issue of fact, asserting a cause and effect relationship, declaring the value of some entity, or advocating a solution to a problem; but, in each case, after you read the argument, you should be able to restate or summarize the position, claim, or thesis in one or two sentences.
- An audience. To evaluate an argument, you need to know the original intended audience or place of publication, so that you can decide if the argument takes into account the audience's attitudes, background, and other factors. Ask yourself, for example, if the writer is assuming too much or too little background knowledge on the part of the audience or if the writer is using language that assumes the reader's agreement on the issue when that assumption is not warranted.
- Evidence from reliable sources. Quotes, statistics, and other evidence should be credited to reputable sources, even if your text is not a document that offers academic-style citations. The evidence should be sufficient to support the author's position or thesis.
- Acknowledgment of the opposing argument. A good rhetorician does not ignore any potential weaknesses in the argument. It is better to acknowledge points in favor of the opposing argument and then, if possible, refute the opposition's strong points than it is to allow an audience to poke holes in an argument.
- A conclusion and/or call to action. An argument can be concluded in a variety of effective ways, but it is important to note that it does, indeed, conclude. The conclusion can be a call to action on the part of the audience, but it should not be the beginning of an additional argument that is not supported by the evidence presented.

ACTIVITY
2.1   ANALYZE A SPEECH OR OTHER PUBLISHED TEXT

As your instructor directs, discuss point-by-point whether the "President-Elect Victory Speech" satisfies the criteria above for the essential elements of an argument.

CLOSE READING OF A TEXT

Rhetorical reading involves careful and patient attention to the text, even reading the text several times. Following are several strategies for reading critically. You do not need to do all of the reading strategies suggested for each essay you read, but as you begin to read critically, you should try all of the strategies at least once to see which strategies supplement your natural reading and learning style.

1. **Learn about the author.** Knowing whether an author is a biologist, a professional writer, or a politician can guide your expectations of the essay. For example, go back to "Smokers Get a Raw Deal" in Chapter 1 and reread the headnote. How does your knowledge that the author was a vice president and director of corporate affairs at Phillip Morris Inc., a tobacco company, affect your trust in him, your belief in his claims, or what you infer is his purpose for writing? If you are reading in a magazine or journal, you can often discover information in the contributor's notes at the beginning or end of the essay or at the beginning or end of the magazine. Many books have a dust jacket or a page giving a short biography of the author. As you learn about the author, jot down any impressions you may have about the author's purpose in writing the essay. Does the author have an obvious agenda in promoting a certain viewpoint on the topic?

2. **Skim the text.** Once you've gotten to know the author a little, it is helpful to read the essay quickly and superficially by reading the introduction, the first sentence in every paragraph, and the conclusion. Read quickly. When you skim a text, you are not trying to understand it. You are preparing for the more careful read that will follow. If the essay tells a story, skimming will give you a good sense of the chronology of the story. When is the story taking place? How much time seems to pass? If the essay is argumentative, skimming will provide

knowledge of the basic structure of the argument and will introduce you to the main points of support. If the essay is primarily informative, you will learn some of the important distinctions and classifications the author uses to organize the information.

It may be interesting to note whether you can get the gist of the reading by skimming. Has the writer provided topic sentences for paragraphs or sections? If so, the writer is trying to make his or her message easily accessible.

3. **Explore your own knowledge and beliefs on the subject.** Make a list of what you already know about the topic of the text. Then make a list of what you believe about this topic. Finally, make a note beside each entry that marks where that information or belief came from.

4. **Reflect on the topic.** The final step before reading is reflecting on what you expect from the essay before you begin a careful reading. What does the title lead you to expect from the essay? Does your quick glance at the essay seem to support the title? How do you feel about the essay so far? Does it anger you, interest you, bore you? Do you think you have any experience that relates to the essay? Will your experience and the author's experience lead you to the same conclusions? One effective way to reflect is to freewrite on the topic of the essay. Exploring what you know before you embark on a careful reading of the essay can deepen your responses.

5. **Annotate**. Read the essay slowly, thinking about what meaning the author is trying to convey to you. It is a good idea to annotate as you read, particularly points that seem important and/or raise questions in your mind. If you don't want to write in your text, try photocopying assigned essays so you can annotate them. You'll probably develop your own system of annotation as you begin to use this technique more often, but here are some basic guidelines to help you begin your annotations:

- Underline sentences, phrases, and words that seem important to the essay.
- Circle words you don't know but think you understand from the context. Then you can look them up later to see if the dictionary definition matches the definition you assumed from the context.
- Write questions in the margins. If the margins aren't large enough to write a complete question, a couple of words to remind you of what you were thinking and a question mark will do. You can also

write brief comments in the margins, again just a few words to remind you of your thoughts.

- Number or put check marks in the margin by major points. Careful annotation of each point in the margin will help you later if you choose to outline.
- Use arrows, lines, and symbols in the margins to connect ideas in the essay that seem related or depend on each other.
- Note transitions, sentence structures, examples, topic sentences, and other rhetorical moves that seem particularly effective in the essay by writing a brief comment or an exclamation mark in the margin next to the underlined text.

This election had many firsts and many stories that will be told for generations. But one that's on my mind tonight's about a woman who cast her ballot in Atlanta. She's a lot like the millions of others who stood in line to make their voice heard in this election except for one thing: Ann Nixon Cooper is 106 years old.

why did he pick her?

After Civil War

Why did skin color prevent vote?

She was born just a generation past slavery; a time when there were no cars on the road or planes in the sky; when someone like her couldn't vote for two reasons: because she was a woman and because of the color of her skin.

And tonight, I think about all that she's seen throughout her century in America -- the heartache and the hope; the struggle and the progress; the times we were told that we can't, and the people who pressed on with that American creed: Yes we can.

Yes We Can

repeats

At a time when women's voices were silenced and their hopes dismissed, she lived to see them stand up and speak out and reach for the ballot: Yes we can

women's rights ①

When there was despair in the dust bowl and depression across the land, she saw a nation conquer fear itself with a New Deal, new jobs, a new sense of common purpose: Yes we can.

depression ②

When the bombs fell on our harbor and tyranny threatened the world, she was there to witness a generation rise to greatness and a democracy was saved: Yes we can

WWII ③

She was there for the buses in Montgomery, the hoses in Birmingham, a bridge in Selma, and a preacher from Atlanta who told a people that "we shall overcome": Yes we can

m.L. King ④

A man touched down on the moon, a wall came down in Berlin, a world was connected by our own science and imagination.

Internet ⑤

And this year, in this election, she touched her finger to a screen, and cast her vote, because after 106 years in America, through the best of times and the darkest of hours, she knows how America can change: Yes we can

America changes

America repeats

In this sidebar, the portion of Barack Obama's speech that focuses upon Ann Nixon Cooper is annotated to show a student's questions, Obama's list of what Ms. Cooper has experienced in her lifetime, and the repetition of the phrase "Yes we can" and the word "America."

Sample Annotated Essay Page

6. **Outline.** An excellent way to distill the meaning of a text is to create an informal outline of the argument. If, as part of annotating the essay, you jot down the main subject of each paragraph in the margin, this will allow you to see the organization of the essay and outline it easily. An outline should list the focus of the essay and track how that focus unfolds paragraph by paragraph. If you are outlining a narrative essay, the outline will probably follow the chronology of the events. Outlining an informative essay, you might find that the outline tracks the steps of a process or reveals divisions and classifications. Outlining an argumentative essay, you'll probably find your outline works to prove a thesis by making statements which support that thesis, raising objections and refuting them, or, perhaps, proposing solutions to solve a problem.

7. **Freewrite about the text.** Another way to distill the meaning of a text is, after you have read it carefully, lay the essay aside, and freewrite for a few minutes about the content and purpose of the essay. If you have not tried freewriting before, it is easy. You simply put your pen to the paper, focus the topic in your mind, and write whatever comes to mind about the topic for a set period of time, perhaps five minutes. If you cannot think of anything to write, you write, "I can't think of anything to write," and then you continue writing what is in your mind. You may find it helpful to begin your freewriting by writing, "This essay is about..." and continue writing, explaining to yourself what you think the essay was about.

8. **Summarize the text**. Write a summary of what you consider to be the primary meaning of the text. Your summary should answer these questions about claims, support, purpose, and audience:
   - What is the author of the essay trying to show or prove (claim)?
   - What does the writer use to convince me that he or she is well informed or right (support)?
   - Why did the writer choose to write this essay (purpose)?
   - Who is the author addressing or writing for (audience)?
   - To write a clear summary, you have to understand the essay. You might test your understanding by reading the essay again and deciding whether your summary is accurate. Writing summaries helps you understand your assignments and prepares you for the numerous summaries you will complete for your research paper.

Responding to Oral and Visual Media

Increasingly, young "politically-minded viewers" are plugging into YouTube, Facebook and comedy shows like "The Daily Show," and other alternative media instead of traditional news outlets. According to a *New York Times* article, surveys and interviews indicated that during the 2008 presidential election "younger voters tend to be not just consumers of news and current events but conduits as well—sending out e-mailed links and videos to friends and their social networks. And in turn, they rely on friends and online connections for news to come to them." **Word of mouth** (via email) is replacing traditional media as the major news filter, at least for young viewers. In this new process, moreover, "viewers" or "writers of email" move seamlessly back and forth between email, text-messaging, television viewing, and Internet surfing, appreciating and sharing the choicest rhetorical pieces with others. "We're talking about a generation that doesn't just like seeing the video in addition to the story—they expect it," said Danny Shea, 23, the associate media editor for *The Huffington Post* (huffingtonpost.com). "And they'll find it elsewhere if you don't give it to them, and then that's the link that's going to be passed around over e-mail and instant message." This multistream, cross-platform method of communication among younger viewers/readers is a fertile forum for rhetorical analysis.

Actually, the lines between oral, written, and visual "texts" have always been somewhat blurred. Speeches delivered orally in person or on television have a visual component, as the audience sees the speaker present the text. A written text is also, in a sense, visual because the audience's mind must process the little squiggles of ink on paper or the computer screen into words. A visual text such as an advertisement or cartoon often includes written text, and, even if it does not, the image will inspire thoughts that are often distilled into language for expression. Reasonably, many of the same techniques used to analyze written and oral texts can also be applied to visual media (cartoons, advertisements, television, etc.).

Responding to Music Lyrics

Music lyrics are performance texts, just as are speeches. They are written to be heard, not written to be read. However, you can analyze the argument in song lyrics such as "Everybody Knows," reprinted below, which was co-written by Leonard Cohen and Sharon Robinson. The song became popular with younger audiences when it was featured in the 1990 film *Pump Up the Volume*. To analyze the song's lyrics rhetorically, you can consider whether the lyrics have a debatable issue, a clear thesis or claim, evidence to support that claim, a particular audience, and a conclusion. For example, is it a debatable issue whether "everybody" knows that people cheat, and that, metaphorically, "the boat is leaking"? With a song, moreover, you can also consider the impact of the lyrics as they are presented by a vocalist accompanied by musical instruments. How does the musical presentation of the lyrics affect their impact as an argument?

"EVERYBODY KNOWS"
By Leonard Cohen and Sharon Robinson.

Everybody knows that the dice are loaded
Everybody rolls with their fingers crossed
Everybody knows that the war is over
Everybody knows the good guys lost
Everybody knows the fight was fixed
The poor stay poor, the rich get rich
That's how it goes
Everybody knows

Everybody knows that the boat is leaking
Everybody knows that the captain lied
Everybody got this broken feeling
Like their father or their dog just died

Everybody talking to their pockets
Everybody wants a box of chocolates
And a long stem rose
Everybody knows

Everybody knows that you love me baby
Everybody knows that you really do
Everybody knows that you've been faithful
Ah give or take a night or two
Everybody knows you've been discreet

But there were so many people you just had to meet
Without your clothes
And everybody knows

Everybody knows, everybody knows
That's how it goes
Everybody knows

Everybody knows, everybody knows
That's how it goes
Everybody knows

And everybody knows that it's now or never
Everybody knows that it's me or you
And everybody knows that you live forever
Ah when you've done a line or two
Everybody knows the deal is rotten
Old black joe's still pickin' cotton
For your ribbons and bows
And everybody knows

And everybody knows that the plague is coming
Everybody knows that it's moving fast
Everybody knows that the naked man and woman
Are just a shining artifact of the past
Everybody knows the scene is dead
But there's gonna be a meter on your bed
That will disclose
What everybody knows

And everybody knows that you're in trouble
Everybody knows what you've been through
From the bloody cross on top of Calvary
To the beach of Malibu
Everybody knows its coming apart
Take one last look at this sacred heart
Before it blows
And everybody knows

Everybody knows, everybody knows
That's how it goes
Everybody knows

Oh everybody knows, everybody knows
That's how it goes
Everybody knows

Everybody knows

ASSIGNMENT:
CONSIDER A SONG AS AN ARGUMENT

Locate a recording of "Everybody Knows" on the Internet and listen to the musical presentation of the song. Then consider the criteria for an argument mentioned above and discuss in your group whether Leonard Cohen and Sharon Robinson make a convincing argument in their song.

RESPONDING TO VISUAL RHETORIC

Methods of analyzing visual rhetoric draw upon several theoretical traditions. In art criticism, viewers may look for symbolism in an image or consider what meaning the artist was trying to convey. Semiotics views images as having intertextuality, as similar images come to have similar meanings, and those meanings may create similar emotions in the viewer. Rhetoricians, as you might expect, consider the argument that an image may present to a viewer. They think about how the subject of the image is presented in relation to other elements in the visual, how the image is cropped, and what lighting and colors are present. Rhetoricians also pay particular attention to the interplay between the visual image and any text that may appear with the image and how the two together construct an argument.

In the following image, a BMW advertisement, for example, a beautiful blond-haired young woman is presented without clothes and lying down with her hair artfully arranged in waves. *Salon* magazine reprinted a copy of the BMW advertisement, pointing out that "in small print scrawled across her

You know you're not the first.

Courtesy BMW premium advertising.

bare shoulder, it reads: 'You know you're not the first.' As your eyes drift to the bottom of the advertisement—and the top of her chest—you learn that it's an advertisement for BMW's premium selection of used cars."

Of course, sexual appeal has been used for decades to sell a whole range of products. However, what do you think is BMW's argument here? *Salon* thinks the ad is implying "Used cars, used women" and that the ad gives a "whole new meaning" to BMW's slogan, printed in the ad: "Sheer Driving Pleasure."

In the image on the next page, Toyota doesn't advertise a car, truck, or any other vehicle. Instead, they advertise the company, saying "We are committed to preserving the delicate balance between man and nature." And, if you look closer, you see that the tree is composed of intertwined humans,

Courtesy Toyota

attached to branches and leaves. The fine print reads, "We've come a long way since we launched our first hybrid car 10 years ago. But our goal goes beyond reducing exhaust emissions. We apply innovative environmental solutions to every aspect of the vehicle's life cycle: from design, manufacture and use, right though to recycling. It's the only way to reach our ultimate aim: zero emissions." Apparently, Toyota doesn't believe that sexy sells cars. Environmental consciousness does.

ACTIVITY
2.2
INTERPRET AN ADVERTISEMENT

Consider the BMW and Toyota advertisements above carefully, first looking only at the images—the beautiful young woman and the tree composed of intertwined human forms. Then consider the images along with the text. In your group discuss these points:

- What is the symbolism of a beautiful young woman (presumably naked) posed as she is in the image?
- What meaning do you think the tag line "You know you're not the first" adds to the image? Then, when you realize the image is an ad for BMW used cars, what do you think?
- What argument is the advertisement making? Can you state the argument in a thesis or purpose statement?
- What about the intertwined and sexless human forms in the Toyota ads? Do you find their connection to the branches and leaves appealing or disturbing?
- Toyota has stated their argument in the text. Does the image match the stated argument?
- Do you find the advertisements amusing, objectionable, or appealing? Do they make you want to buy a used BMW or a Toyota vehicle?

Combining Articles and Images

Many of the texts we encounter in everyday life—in newspapers, magazines, and on the Internet—are not texts in isolation but, are texts combined with images. Indeed, when readers first glance at one of these media, likely their attention is caught first by photos, then by headlines. Only after being engaged by these attention-getting visual elements (for headlines are visual elements as well as written) are readers likely to focus on written text. Student writers today, like professionals, have access to the use of visual elements in their compositions, and adding photos can not only catch reader attention but also emphasize particular points of an argument or create an overall mood.

The article "A Couple in Chicago," published in the *New Yorker* online in 2009, was part of a 1996 photo essay project by photographer Mariana Cook and is accompanied by an excerpt from her interviews with Barack and Michelle Obama in which they discuss a possible interest in politics. Notice that the headline says merely, "A Couple in Chicago." Probably, you looked at the photos for a second or two before realizing that the Chicago couple is, in fact, the president and first lady, though in younger days.

Cook says on her website of her photo portraits that she likes to use natural light and tries, as much as possible, to allow her subjects to forget they are being photographed: "It is fortunate and almost magical when the psychological qualities of a person are integrated and made evident in a fraction of a second."

Remember the context of the Obamas' photos and text: they were photographed and interviewed in 1996 when they were relatively unknown, before Barack Obama became a best-selling author or senator. If you had come upon these photos and text before you had ever heard of the couple, what impression would the photos give you? The portrait of the Obamas as a couple is a very relaxed image in which they sit closely on the sofa of their home, seemingly almost a candid shot taken by a family friend. Their comments also convey a relaxed, candid, and optimistic attitude that matches the tone set by the photos. However, coming upon the photos now, after all the publicity and hype about the Obamas, what impression do the images and text convey to you?

**READING
2.2**

"A COUPLE IN CHICAGO"

THE NEW YORKER

REPORTING & ESSAYS | ARTS & CULTURE | HUMOR | FICTION & POETRY | THE TALK OF THE TOWN | ONLINE ONLY

THE POLITICAL
SCENE
Obamanomics and the
President's budget initiatives.

BLOGS

Steve Coll digs into stimulus
defense spending.

Hendrik Hertzberg laughs at
"economic fascism."

Evan Osnos thinks China is
winning the race to be green.

News Desk: Detroit in three
acts.

Sasha Frere-Jones
recommends a documentary
about Gorillaz.

James Surowiecki charts the
stock market's long, strange trip.

George Packer connects "Little
Dorrit" to "The Wire."

The Book Bench: Shawn
Mortensen.

The Front Row: Forget "The
Wrestler." Get ready for "The
Fighter."

The Cartoon Lounge:
Homemade office bots.

Goings On: When is a four-star
review negative?

SEE ALL BLOG POSTS

THE
BOOK CLUB
Read "Down and Out in Paris
and London" with *The New
Yorker.*

IN THIS
ISSUE
View the **table of contents.**

COVERS
Browse the complete archive
using the cover gallery.

Select a year ▾

PORTFOLIO

A COUPLE IN CHICAGO

by Mariana Cook

TEXT SIZE: A | A | A
PRINT | E-MAIL | FEEDS

JANUARY 19, 2009

RELATED LINKS
Mariana Cook's official Web
site

KEYWORDS
(Pres.) Barack Obama;
Michelle Obama; Marriage;
Politics; Presidents; First
Ladies; Relationships

*On May 26, 1996, Mariana Cook visited
Barack and Michelle Obama in Hyde Park as
part of a photography project on couples in
America. What follows is excerpted from her
interviews with them.*

MICHELLE OBAMA: There is a strong
possibility that Barack will pursue a political
career, although it's unclear. There is a little
tension with that. I'm very wary of politics. I
think he's too much of a good guy for the kind of brutality, the skepticism.

When you are involved in politics, your life is an open book, and people can
come in who don't necessarily have good intent. I'm pretty private, and like to
surround myself with people that I trust and love. In politics you've got to open
yourself to a lot of different people. There is a possibility that our futures will go
that way, even though I want to have kids and travel, spend time with family, and
like spending time with friends. But we are going to be busy people doing lots of

stuff. And it'll be interesting to see what life has to offer. In many ways, we are here for the ride, just sort of seeing what opportunities open themselves up. And the more you experiment the easier it is to do different things. If I had stayed in a law firm and made partner, my life would be completely different. I wouldn't know the people I know, and I would be more risk-averse. Barack has helped me loosen up and feel comfortable with taking risks, not doing things the traditional way and sort of testing it out, because that is how he grew up. I'm more traditional; he's the one in the couple that, I think, is the less traditional individual. You can probably tell from the photographs—he's just more out there, more flamboyant. I'm more, like, "Well, let's wait and see. What did that look like? How much does it weigh?"

BARACK OBAMA: All my life, I have been stitching together a family, through stories or memories or friends or ideas. Michelle has had a very different background—very stable, two-parent family, mother at home, brother and dog, living in the same house all their lives. We represent two strands of family life in this country—the strand that is very stable and solid, and then the strand that is breaking out of the constraints of traditional families, travelling, separated, mobile. I think there was that strand in me of imagining what it would be like to have a stable, solid, secure family life.

Michelle is a tremendously strong person, and has a very strong sense of herself and who she is and where she comes from. But I also think in her eyes you can see a trace of vulnerability that most people don't know, because when she's walking through the world she is this tall, beautiful, confident woman. There is a part of her that is vulnerable and young and sometimes frightened, and I think seeing both of those things is what attracted me to her. And then what sustains our relationship is I'm extremely happy with her, and part of it has to do with the fact that she is at once completely familiar to me, so that I can be myself and she knows me very well and I trust her completely, but at the same time she is also a complete mystery to me in some ways. And there are times when we are lying in bed and I look over and sort of have a start. Because I realize here is this other person who is separate and different and has different memories and backgrounds and thoughts and feelings. It's that tension between familiarity and mystery that makes for something strong, because, even as you build a life of trust and comfort and mutual support, you retain some sense of surprise or wonder about the other person. ♦

ACTIVITY 2.3   ANALYZE INTERACTIONS OF TEXT AND IMAGES

Locate a newspaper or magazine article or a website in which the photo or photos and the text complement or enhance each other. Bring your example to class and discuss the interrelationship between text and image. Likely, the images catch your attention first and make a certain impression. Then, when you read the accompanying article, that impression is amplified. Thus, the image affects the reader's impression of the text which may, in turn, cause a re-evaluation of the images.

ACTIVITY 2.4   READING JOURNAL

As you analyze a speech, essay, song, or visual you may find yourself relating to the text in personal ways. You may agree or disagree with particular parts, and some things about the "text" may remind you of events that have happened in your own life. In most cases you can't actually sit down and talk with the author or artist, but you can keep a reading journal to record your thoughts and impressions. A reading journal can be kept either in a notebook or as entries submitted to the class online discussion board. As your instructor requests, complete one or more of the following statements about one of the "texts" in this chapter and then elaborate on your answer:

"I feel the author (or artist) is trying to . . ."

"The most interesting thing about this 'text' was . . ."

"The most significant question raised is . . ."

"I agree with the writer (or artist) about . . ."

"I disagree with the writer (or artist) about . . ."

"I wish I could tell the author (or artist)…"

three

3

RHETORICAL ARGUMENTS SURVIVE THE TEST OF TIME

The Declaration of Independence is not only an historical document; its assertions serve as a benchmark for the status of freedom in the United States and in countries around the world. For example, Dr. Martin Luther King, Jr. stood in front of a crowd of thousands at the Lincoln memorial in 1963 to present his "I Have a Dream" speech, reprinted in Chapter 4, which refers specifically to the Declaration of Independence. He said,

> When the architects of our republic wrote the magnificent words of the Constitution and the Declaration of Independence, they were signing a promissory note to which every American was to fall heir. This note was a promise that all men, yes, black men as well as white men, would be guaranteed the "unalienable Rights" of "Life, Liberty and the pursuit of Happiness." It is obvious today that America has defaulted on this promissory note, insofar as her citizens of color are concerned. Instead of honoring this sacred obligation, America has given the Negro people a bad check, a check which has come back marked "insufficient funds."

According to Dr. King, America had not lived up to the promise made in the Declaration of Independence that all men were created equal and entitled to the "unalienable Rights" of "Life, Liberty and the pursuit of Happiness." But King was not content with blame and accusations; he had a dream that America would someday make good on that "bad check" and that Negro people would be equal to whites.

Then, in November 2008, President-Elect Barack Obama stood in front of another crowd of thousands as he gave the "Victory Speech," which you have just read in Chapter 2, and reminded America that the "preacher from Atlanta" [King] had said, "We will overcome [prejudice]." Just by his physical presence as an African-American president-elect, Obama evoked the heritage both of King's speech and of the Declaration of Independence. Obama said, "If there is anyone out there who still doubts that America is a place where all things are possible; who still wonders if the dream of our founders is alive in our time; who still questions the power of our democracy, tonight is your answer."

The Declaration of Independence, as author Stephen E. Lucas shows in the following document, brilliantly served its purpose of declaring the independence of the 13 American colonies. Moreover, as the examples from the speeches by President-Elect Obama and Dr. King attest, the Declaration has stood the test of time and is still relevant in asserting the occasion and the necessity for the nation's freedom and equality.

READING 3.1

"THE STYLISTIC ARTISTRY OF THE DECLARATION OF INDEPENDENCE" BY STEPHEN E. LUCAS

The article by Stephen E. Lucas, author of The Art of Public Speaking, *analyzes the structure, content, and style of the Declaration of Independence. The National Archives and Records Administration, which cares for the most important historical United States documents, includes the following reading on its website. Only the first part of Lucas's article is reprinted here, the part reviewing the introduction, which establishes the "necessity" of independence, and the preamble, which includes the most famous and often quoted parts of the Declaration. The remaining two-thirds of the document, that is not included, is primarily a detailed attack on the treatment of the American Colonies by George III, essential evidence to the 18th century audience who needed to be assured that all other options short of independence had been tried without success. However, the latter part of the document receives less attention today.*

The Declaration of Independence is perhaps the most masterfully written state paper of Western civilization. As Moses Coit Tyler noted almost a century ago, no assessment of it can be complete without taking into account its extraordinary merits as a work of political prose style. Although many scholars have recognized those merits, there are surprisingly few sustained studies of the stylistic artistry of the Declaration.(1) This essay seeks to illuminate that artistry by probing the discourse microscopically—at the level of the sentence, phrase, word, and syllable. By approaching the Declaration in this way, we can shed light both on its literary qualities and on its rhetorical power as a work designed to convince a "candid world" that the American colonies were justified in seeking to establish themselves as an independent nation.(2)

The text of the Declaration can be divided into five sections—the introduction, the preamble, the indictment of George III, the denunciation of the British people, and the conclusion. Because space does not permit us to explicate each section in full detail, we shall select features from each that illustrate the stylistic artistry of the Declaration as a whole.(3)

The introduction consists of the first paragraph—a single, lengthy, periodic sentence:

> **When in the Course of human events, it becomes necessary for one people to dissolve the political bands which have connected them with another, and to assume among the powers of the earth, the separate and equal station to which the Laws of Nature and of Nature's God entitle them, a decent respect to the opinions of mankind requires that they should declare the causes which impel them to the separation.(4)**

Taken out of context, this sentence is so general it could be used as the introduction to a declaration by any "oppressed" people. Seen within its original context, however, it is a model of subtlety, nuance, and implication that works on several levels of meaning and allusion to orient readers toward a favorable view of America and to prepare them for the rest of the Declaration. From its magisterial opening phrase, which sets the American Revolution within the whole "course of human events," to its assertion that "the Laws of Nature and of Nature's God" entitle America to a "separate and equal station among the powers of the earth," to its quest for sanction from "the opinions of mankind," the introduction elevates the quarrel with England from a petty political dispute to a major event in the grand sweep of history. It dignifies the Revolution as a contest of principle and implies that the American cause has a special claim to moral legitimacy—all without mentioning England or America by name.

Rather than defining the Declaration's task as one of persuasion, which would doubtless raise the defenses of readers as well as imply that there was more than one publicly credible view of the British-American conflict, the introduction identifies the purpose of the Declaration as simply to "declare"—to announce publicly in explicit terms—the "causes" impelling America to leave the British empire. This gives the Declaration, at the outset, an aura of philosophical (in the eighteenth-century sense of the term) objectivity that it will seek to maintain throughout. Rather than presenting one side in a public controversy on which good and decent people could differ, the Declaration purports to do no more than a natural philosopher would do in reporting the causes of any physical event. The issue, it implies, is not one of interpretation but of observation.

The most important word in the introduction is "necessary," which in the eighteenth century carried strongly deterministic overtones. To say an act was necessary implied that it was impelled by fate or determined by the operation of inextricable natural laws and was beyond the control of human agents. Thus Chambers's *Cyclopedia* defined "necessary" as "that which cannot but be, or cannot be otherwise." "The common notion of necessity and impossibility," Jonathan Edwards wrote in *Freedom of the Will*, "implies something that frustrates endeavor or desire. . . . That is necessary in the original and proper sense of the word, which is, or will be, notwithstanding all supposable opposition." Characterizing the Revolution as necessary suggested that it resulted from constraints that operated with lawlike force throughout the material universe and within the sphere of human action. The Revolution was not merely preferable, defensible, or justifiable. It was as inescapable, as inevitable, as unavoidable within the course of human events as the motions of the tides or the changing of the seasons within the course of natural events.(5)

Investing the Revolution with connotations of necessity was particularly important because, according to the law of nations, recourse to war was lawful only when it became "necessary"—only when amicable negotiation had failed and all other alternatives for settling the differences between two states had been exhausted. Nor was the burden of necessity limited to monarchs and established nations. At the start of the English Civil War in 1642, Parliament defended its recourse to military action against Charles I in a lengthy declaration demonstrating the "Necessity to take up Arms." Following this tradition, in July 1775 the Continental Congress issued its own Declaration Setting Forth the Causes and Necessity of Their Taking Up Arms. When, a year later, Congress decided the colonies could no longer retain their liberty within the British empire, it adhered to long-established rhetorical convention by describing independence as a matter of absolute and inescapable necessity.(6) Indeed, the notion of necessity was so important that in addition to appearing in the introduction of the Declaration, it was invoked twice more at crucial junctures in the rest of the text and appeared frequently in other congressional papers after July 4, 1776.(7)

Labeling the Americans "one people" and the British "another" was also laden with implication and performed several important strategic functions within the Declaration. First, because two alien peoples cannot be made one, it reinforced the notion that breaking the "political bands" with England was a necessary step in the course of human events. America and England were already separated by the more basic fact that they had become two different peoples. The gulf between them was much more than political; it was intellectual, social, moral, cultural and, according to the principles of nature, could no more be repaired, as Thomas Paine said, than one could "restore to us the time that is past" or "give to prostitution its former innocence." To try to perpetuate a purely political connection would be "forced and unnatural," "repugnant to reason, to the universal order of things."(8)

Second, once it is granted that Americans and Englishmen are two distinct peoples, the conflict between them is less likely to be seen as a civil war. The Continental Congress knew America could not withstand Britain's military might without foreign assistance. But they also knew America could not receive assistance as long as the colonies were fighting a civil war as part of the British empire. To help the colonies would constitute interference in Great Britain's internal affairs. As Samuel Adams explained, "no foreign Power can consistently yield Comfort to Rebels, or enter into any kind of Treaty with these Colonies till they declare themselves free and independent." The crucial factor in opening the way for foreign aid was the act of declaring independence. But by defining America and England as two separate peoples, the Declaration reinforced the perception that the conflict was not a civil war, thereby, as Congress noted in its debates on independence, making it more "consistent with European delicacy for European powers to treat with us, or even to receive an Ambassador."(9)

Third, defining the Americans as a separate people in the introduction eased the task of invoking the right of revolution in the preamble. That right, according to eighteenth-century revolutionary principles, could be invoked only in the most dire of circumstances—when "resistance was absolutely necessary in order to preserve the nation from slavery, misery, and ruin"—and then only by "the Body of the People." If America and Great Britain were seen as one people, Congress could not justify revolution against the British government for the simple reason that the body of the people (of which the Americans would be only one part) did not support the American cause. For America to move against the government in such circumstances would not be a justifiable act of resistance but "a sort of Sedition, Tumult, and War . . . aiming only at the satisfaction of private Lust, without regard to the public Good." By defining the Americans as a separate people, Congress could more readily satisfy the requirement for invoking the right of revolution that "the whole Body of Subjects" rise up against the government "to rescue themselves from the most violent and illegal oppressions."(10)

Like the introduction, the next section of the Declaration—usually referred to as the preamble—is universal in tone and scope. It contains no explicit reference to the British-American conflict, but outlines a general philosophy of government that makes revolution justifiable, even meritorious:

> **We hold these truths to be self-evident, that all men are created equal, that they are endowed by their Creator with certain unalienable Rights, that among these are Life, Liberty and the pursuit of Happiness. That to secure these rights, Governments are instituted among Men, deriving their just powers from the consent of the governed. That whenever any Form of Government becomes destructive of these ends, it is the Right of the People to alter or to abolish it, and to institute new Government, laying its foundation on such principles and organizing its powers in such form, as to them shall seem most likely to effect their Safety and Happiness. Prudence, indeed, will dictate that Governments long established should not be changed for light and transient causes; and accordingly all experience hath shown that mankind are more disposed to suffer, while evils are sufferable, than to right themselves by abolishing the forms to which they are accustomed. But when a long train of abuses and usurpations, pursuing invariably the same Object evinces a design to reduce them under absolute Despotism, it is their right, it is their duty, to throw off such Government, and to provide new Guards for their future security.**

Like the rest of the Declaration, the preamble is "brief, free of verbiage, a model of clear, concise, simple statement."(11) It capsulizes in five sentences—202—words what it took John Locke thousands of words to explain in his Second Treatise of Government. Each word is chosen and placed to achieve maximum impact. Each clause is indispensable to the progression of thought. Each sentence is carefully constructed internally and in relation to what precedes and follows. In its ability to compress complex ideas into a brief, clear statement, the preamble is a paradigm of eighteenth-century Enlightenment prose style, in which purity, simplicity, directness, precision, and, above all, perspicuity were the highest rhetorical and literary virtues. One word follows another with complete inevitability of sound and meaning. Not one word can be moved or replaced without disrupting the balance and harmony of the entire preamble.

The stately and dignified tone of the preamble—like that of the introduction—comes partly from what the eighteenth century called Style Periodique, in which, as Hugh Blair explained in his *Lectures on Rhetoric and Belles Lettres*, "the sentences are composed of several members linked together, and hanging upon one another, so that the sense of the whole is not brought out till the close." This, Blair said, "is the most pompous, musical, and oratorical manner of composing" and "gives an air of gravity and dignity to composition." The gravity and dignity of the preamble were reinforced by its conformance with the rhetorical precept that "when we aim at dignity or elevation, the sound [of each sentence] should be made to grow to the last; the longest members of the period, and the fullest and most sonorous words, should be reserved to the conclusion." None of the sentences of the preamble end on a single-syllable word; only one, the second (and least euphonious), ends on a two-syllable word. Of the other four, one ends with a four-syllable word ("security"), while three end with three-syllable words. Moreover, in each of the three-syllable words the closing syllable is at least a medium-length four-letter syllable, which helps bring the sentences to "a full and harmonious close."(12)

It is unlikely that any of this was accidental. Thoroughly versed in classical oratory and rhetorical theory as well as in the belletristic treatises of his own time, Thomas Jefferson, draftsman of the Declaration, was a diligent student of rhythm, accent, timing, and cadence in discourse. This can be seen most clearly in his "Thoughts on English Prosody," a remarkable twenty-eight-page unpublished essay written in Paris during the fall of 1786. Prompted by a discussion on language with the Marquis de Chastellux at Monticello four years earlier, it was a careful inquiry designed "to find out the real circumstance which gives harmony to English prose and laws to those who make it." Using roughly the same system of diacritical notation he had employed in 1776 in his reading draft of the Declaration, Jefferson systematically analyzed the patterns of accentuation in a wide range of English writers, including Milton, Pope, Shakespeare, Addison, Gray, and Garth. Although "Thoughts on English Prosody" deals with poetry, it displays Jefferson's keen sense of the interplay between sound and sense in language. There can be little doubt that, like many accomplished writers, he consciously composed for the ear as well as for the eye—a trait that is nowhere better illustrated than in the eloquent cadences of the preamble in the Declaration of Independence.(13)

The preamble also has a powerful sense of structural unity. This is achieved partly by the latent chronological progression of thought, in which the reader is moved from the creation of mankind, to the institution of government, to the throwing off of government when it fails to protect the people's unalienable rights, to the creation of new government that will better secure the people's safety and happiness. This dramatic scenario, with its first act implicitly set in the Garden of Eden (where man was "created equal"), may, for some readers, have contained mythic overtones of humanity's fall from divine grace. At the very least, it gives an almost archetypal quality to the ideas of the preamble and continues the notion, broached in the introduction, that the American Revolution is a major development in "the course of human events."

Because of their concern with the philosophy of the Declaration, many modern scholars have dealt with the opening sentence of the preamble out of context, as if Jefferson and the Continental Congress intended it to stand alone. Seen in context, however, it is part of a series of five propositions that build upon one another through the first three sentences of the preamble to establish the right of revolution against tyrannical authority:

Proposition 1:	All men are created equal.
Proposition 2:	They [all men, from proposition 1] are endowed by their creator with certain unalienable rights
Proposition 3:	Among these [man's unalienable rights, from proposition 2] are life, liberty, and the pursuit of happiness
Proposition 4:	To secure these rights [man's unalienable rights, from propositions 2 and 3] governments are instituted among men

Proposition 5:   Whenever any form of government becomes de-
                 structive of these ends [securing man's unalienable
                 rights, from propositions 2-4], it is the right of the
                 people to alter or to abolish it.

When we look at all five propositions, we see they are meant to be
read together and have been meticulously written to achieve a specific rhetorical purpose. The first three lead into the fourth, which in
turn leads into the fifth. And it is the fifth, proclaiming the right of
revolution when a government becomes destructive of the people's
unalienable rights, that is most crucial in the overall argument of the
Declaration. The first four propositions are merely preliminary steps
designed to give philosophical grounding to the fifth.

Although the preamble is the best known part of the Declaration today, it attracted considerably less attention in its own time. For most
eighteenth-century readers, it was an unobjectionable statement of
commonplace political principles. As Jefferson explained years later,
the purpose of the Declaration was "not to find out new principles, or
new arguments, never before thought of . . . but to place before mankind the common sense of the subject, in terms so plain and firm as
to command their assent, and to justify ourselves in the independent
stand we are compelled to take."(14)

Far from being a weakness of the preamble, the lack of new ideas
was perhaps its greatest strength. If one overlooks the introductory
first paragraph, the Declaration as a whole is structured along the
lines of a deductive argument that can easily be put in syllogistic
form:

    Major premise: When government deliberately seeks to reduce the
                        people under absolute despotism, the people have
                        a right, indeed a duty, to alter or abolish that form
                        of government and to create new guards for their
                        future security.
    Minor premise: The government of Great Britain has deliberately
                        sought to reduce the American people under
                        absolute despotism.

| Conclusion: | Therefore the American people have a right, indeed a duty, to abolish their present form of government and to create new guards for their future security. |

As the major premise in this argument, the preamble allowed Jefferson and the Congress to reason from self-evident principles of government accepted by almost all eighteenth-century readers of the Declaration.(15)

The key premise, however, was the minor premise. Since virtually everyone agreed the people had a right to overthrow a tyrannical ruler when all other remedies had failed, the crucial question in July 1776 was whether the necessary conditions for revolution existed in the colonies. Congress answered this question with a sustained attack on George III, an attack that makes up almost exactly two-thirds of the text [of the Declaration of Independence].

ACTIVITY 3.1
ANALYZE THE RHETORICAL ARGUMENTS

1. Locate the part of Stephen E. Lucas's article that analyzes the preamble, particularly the part which Dr. Martin Luther King, Jr., referred to, specifically this sentence: "We hold these truths to be self-evident, that all men are created equal, that they are endowed by their Creator with certain unalienable Rights, that among these are Life, Liberty and the pursuit of Happiness." Dr. King called this part of the Declaration of Independence a "promissory note," and said "It is obvious today that America has defaulted on this promissory note, insofar as her citizens of color are concerned." Why did he say that and what did he mean?

2. President-Elect Obama opened his "Victory Speech" with a sentence which also referred to the first sentence in the Preamble of the Declaration of Independence, "If there is anyone out there who still doubts that America is a place where all things are possible; who still wonders if the dream of our founders is alive in our time; who still questions the power

of our democracy, tonight is your answer." What did President Obama mean?

3. Perhaps surprisingly, Lucas writes about the statement that "all men are created equal," [M}any modern scholars have dealt with the opening sentence of the preamble out of context, as if Jefferson and the Continental Congress intended it to stand alone. What does Lucas say that Jefferson and the Continental Congress intended by the preamble? Why do you think that the opening sentence receives more attention today than it did at the time of its writing?

THE RHETORICAL TRIANGLE

The act of speaking or writing encompasses three elements: the writer (or **speaker**), the purpose (or **subject**), and the **audience** (or reader). In the case of the Declaration of Independence, Thomas Jefferson wrote the basic draft, though the document was signed by all the members of the Continental Congress. The purpose of the document was to declare in-

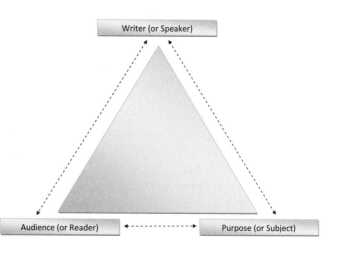

dependence and, as Stephen E. Lucas points out, to show such a declaration was "necessary" or inevitable, given the offenses of the British government. Otherwise, the Americans were merely rebels in a civil war. The document had several immediate audiences—the colonists themselves who may or may not have supported such a declaration, the British government, and foreign powers such as France whom the Continental Congress hoped to entice into entering the war. Without foreign support, the war was likely to fail. Over time, however, the Declaration has acquired other audiences, such as generations of Americans and people around the world who hold the United States accountable for the promises it made when it declared that "all men are created equal, that they are endowed by their Creator with certain unalienable Rights, that among these are Life, Liberty and the pursuit of Happiness."

Like the occasion for the writing of the Declaration of Independence, every speaking or writing situation has the same three elements, though some situations may be more urgent or persuasive than others. A good way to visualize the three interacting rhetorical elements is as a triangle.

The *writer's* or *speaker's* charge is to project an ethos or image of credibility and reliability that is persuasive to the audience. An effective writer is always aware of the *audience's* characteristics, including demographics, level of knowledge about the subject, prejudices, values, and emotions. The writer may inform the reader of information or express thoughts about a topic, but all rhetorical purposes are, in some way, persuasive. For example, Stephen E. Lucas points out that the introduction of the Declaration of Independence identifies the purpose of the Declaration as simply to "declare"—to announce publicly in explicit terms—the "causes" impelling America to leave the British empire. This gives the Declaration, at the outset, an aura of philosophical (in the eighteenth-century sense of the term) objectivity that it will seek to maintain throughout. Rather than presenting one side in a public controversy on which good and decent people could differ, the Declaration purports to do no more than a natural philosopher would do in reporting the causes of any physical event. The issue, it implies, is not one of interpretation but of observation.

So, the Continental Congress may not have voiced their intent to argue independence but to declare it, so that they would not be inviting argument in return. There, indeed, may have been no need to persuade the British of their intent, as fighting had already begun; but no matter what they stated, the signers of the Declaration desperately needed to persuade both American colonists and the French (potential allies) of the seriousness and validity of American independence. By signing their names to the document, members of the Continental Congress thus declared themselves traitors to the British. There was no turning back, for them, or for anyone who supported the cause of American independence.

ARISTOTLE'S PERSUASIVE APPEALS

Some theorists associate the rhetorical triangle directly with Aristotle's **appeals** (or proofs): *ethos, pathos,* and *logos.* **Ethos** refers to the writer's (or speaker's) credibility, **pathos** to emotion used to sway the audience; and, finally, purpose (or subject) to **logos**, for an effective argument will include evidence and other supporting details to back up the author's claims.

Aristotle wrote:
Of those proofs that are furnished through the speech there

are three kinds. Some reside in the character [*ethos*] of the speaker, some in a certain disposition [*pathos*] of the audience and some in the speech itself, through its demonstrating or seeming to demonstrate [*logos*].

Contemporary theorist Wayne C. Booth said something similar: The common ingredient that I find in all writing that I admire—excluding for now novels, plays, and poems—is something that I shall reluctantly call the rhetorical stance, a stance which depends upon discovering and maintaining in any writing situation a proper balance among the three elements that are at work in any communicative effort; the available arguments about the subject itself [*logos*], the interests and peculiarities of the audience [*pathos*], and the voice, the implied character of the speaker [*ethos*].

ARGUMENTS FROM *LOGOS*

Logos or reason was Aristotle's favorite of the three persuasive appeals, and he bemoaned the fact that humans could not be persuaded through reason alone, indeed that they sometimes chose emotion over reason. Aristotle also used the term *logos* to mean rational discourse. To appeal to *logos* means to organize an argument with a clear claim or thesis, supported by logical reasons that are presented in a

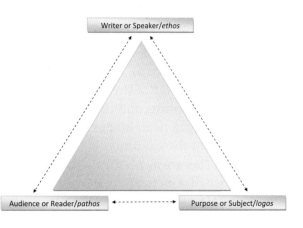

well-organized manner that is internally consistent. It can also mean the use of facts and statistics as evidence. However, logos without elements of pathos and ethos can be dry, hard to understand, and boring.

**READING
3.2**

"LET'S GET RID OF DARWINISM"
BY OLIVIA JUDSON

Olivia Judson is an evolutionary biologist with a doctorate from Oxford. She is also the best-selling author of Dr. Tatiana's Sex Advice to All Creation *which describes the variety of sexual practices in the natural world. This essay was printed as an Op-Ed in the* New York Times.

Charles Darwin was a giant. He did not merely write "On the Origin of Species"—one of the most important books ever written by anyone—in which he describes how evolution by natural selection works, and what some of its consequences and implications are. He also wrote—and this list is not exhaustive—a treatise on the formation of coral reefs that is still thought to be correct; a definitive monograph on barnacles, both extinct and extant; a book about how earthworms make soil; a now-classic text on carnivorous plants (the ones, like Venus fly-traps, that ensnare and digest insects); a book about the strange ways that orchids get themselves fertilized; and an account of the five years he spent aboard the ship HMS Beagle, which has become a classic of travel writing.

As if that wasn't enough, he proposed sexual selection—the idea that decorations and ornaments, like peacocks' tails, evolve because females in many species prefer to mate with the most beautiful males. Sexual selection has since become a major field of research in its own right.

In short, Darwin did more in one lifetime than most of us could hope to accomplish in two. But his giantism has had an odd and problematic consequence. It's a tendency for everyone to refer back to him. "Why Darwin was wrong about X"; "Was Darwin wrong about Y?"; "What Darwin didn't know about Z"—these are common headlines in newspapers and magazines, in both the biological and the general literature. Then there are the words: Darwinism (sometimes used with the prefix "neo"), Darwinist (ditto), Darwinian.

Why is this a problem? Because it's all grossly misleading. It suggests that Darwin was the beginning and the end, the alpha and omega, of evolutionary biology, and that the subject hasn't changed much in the 149 years since the publication of the "Origin."

He wasn't, and it has. Although several of his ideas—natural and sexual selection among them—remain cornerstones of modern evolutionary biology, the field as a whole has been transformed. If we were to go back in a time machine and fetch him to the present day, he'd find much of evolutionary biology unintelligible—at least until he'd had time to study genetics, statistics and computer science.

Oh, there would be so much to tell him! A full list would take me weeks to write out. But the obvious place to begin would be the discoveries of genetics, especially DNA. We'd have to explain that cells in each organism contain a code describing how to build that organism, written in chemical form—DNA—that evolutionary forces are constantly rewriting. Indeed, the study of DNA allows us to see the action of natural selection on a molecule-by-molecule basis. We can see the genes where natural selection acts to prevent evolutionary change, those where it drives change and those where it has no effect at all.

Then there's the fusion of genetics with natural selection, which has enormously expanded our understanding of how natural selection can work. For example, it has led to the discovery that natural selection does not just shape individuals—the length of a beak, the color of a fin. It can also act on family groups, and thus drive the evolution of cooperation and other altruistic behaviors.

The reason is that evolutionary success can now be measured in terms of the number of genes an individual contributes to the next generation. Anyone who dies without reproducing does not directly contribute any. But because individuals have some genes in common with their family members, they can make an indirect genetic contribution if they help their relations to reproduce instead of reproducing themselves. Such "kin selection" is thought to have contributed to the evolution of the social insects—especially, ants, bees, wasps and termites—where only a few individuals reproduce and everyone else looks after the offspring.

We'd want to discuss evolution beyond natural selection—the other forces that can sometimes cause (or prevent) evolutionary change. For although natural selection is the only creative force in evolution—the only one that can produce complex structures such as wings and eyes—it is not the only force that affects which genes will spread, and which will vanish.

And, and, and.

What would he make of it all?

I think his reaction would be a mix of satisfaction and astonishment. Satisfaction: that natural selection has turned out to be such a powerful idea, explaining such a wide range of phenomena. Astonishment: for the same reason. He would, I think, be fascinated by the weird natural history that has been discovered in the past 150 years—such as Wolbachia, bacteria that pervert the reproduction of insects for their own ends. (Wolbachia can have a number of effects, but one of the most common is to kill all a female's sons. The reason is that sons don't transmit Wolbachia, so from Wolbachia's point of view, they are a waste of space.) I'm not sure he'd enjoy analyzing DNA sequences—he might find it a bit too abstracted from the living organism—but I think he'd be delighted to learn the results. I think he would be shocked by how much we know about the so-called model organisms—worms, toads, fruit flies, mice, humans and the bacterium E. coli—and how little we know about everything else. And I think he'd be startled by the nature of scientific research—the scale of the enterprise, the cost, the pressures to publish and the degree of specialization that results. His brand of science—20 years of thinking about a problem before publishing—could not be done today.

But I digress. To return to my argument: I'd like to abolish the insidious terms Darwinism, Darwinist and Darwinian. They suggest a false narrowness to the field of modern evolutionary biology, as though it was the brainchild of a single person 150 years ago, rather than a vast, complex and evolving subject to which many other great figures have contributed. (The science would be in a sorry state if one man 150 years ago had, in fact, discovered everything there was to say.) Obsessively focusing on Darwin, perpetually asking whether he was right about this or that, implies that the discovery of something he didn't think of or know about somehow undermines or threatens the whole enterprise of evolutionary biology today.

It does not. In the years ahead, I predict we will continue to refine our understanding of natural selection, and continue to discover new ways in which it can shape genes and genomes. Indeed, as genetic data continues to flood into the databanks, we will be able to ask questions about the detailed workings of evolution that it has not been possible to ask before.

Yet all too often, evolution—insofar as it is taught in biology classes at all—is taught as the story of Charles Darwin. Then the pages are turned, and everyone settles down to learn how the heart works, or how plants make energy from sunshine, or some other detail. The evolutionary concepts that unify biology, that allow us to frame questions and investigate the glorious diversity of life—these are ignored.

Darwin was an amazing man, and the principal founder of evolutionary biology. But his was the first major statement on the subject, not the last. Calling evolutionary biology "Darwinism," and evolution by natural selection "Darwinian" evolution, is like calling aeronautical engineering "Wrightism," and fixed-wing aircraft "Wrightian" planes, after those pioneers of fixed-wing flight, the Wright brothers. The best tribute we could give Darwin is to call him the founder—and leave it at that. Plenty of people in history have had an -ism named after them. Only a handful can claim truly to have given birth to an entire field of modern science.

ACTIVITY 3.2   **ANALYZE AN ARGUMENT FROM *LOGOS***

Olivia Judson in "Let's Get Rid of Darwinism" is essentially arguing against the popular wisdom that Charles Darwin is the beginning and the end, the "alpha and the omega," of evolutionary biology. In your group, answer the following questions.

- Explain how Judson's argument is an appeal to *logos*. Does she offer a clear thesis or claim? Does she offer reasonable evidence to support her thesis?

- Do you think Judson makes a valid argument that evolutionary biology should not be tied to Darwin's fallibility or infallibility? Why or why not?
- In what ways does Judson make use of *pathos* or *ethos* to bolster her argument?

DEDUCTIVE REASONING

Aristotle was the first person in Western culture to write systematically about logic, and he is credited with developing and promoting syllogistic or **deductive reasoning** in which statements are combined to draw a **conclusion**. He wrote that "a statement is persuasive and credible either because it is directly self-evident or because it appears to be proved from other statements that are so." This logical structure is called a **syllogism**, in which premises lead to a conclusion. The following is perhaps the most famous syllogism:

Major premise:	All humans are mortal.
Minor premise:	Socrates is human.
Conclusion:	Socrates is mortal.

The **major premise** is a general statement accepted by everyone which makes an observation about all people. The second statement of the syllogism is the **minor premise** which makes a statement about a particular case within the class of all people. Comparison of the two premises, the general class of "all humans" and the particular case of "Socrates" within the class of "all humans" leads to the conclusion that Socrates also fits in the class "mortal," and thus his death is unavoidable. Thus, the logic moves from the general to the particular.

Similarly, if you try the pumpkin bread at one Starbucks and like it, you infer that you will like the pumpkin bread at another Starbucks. The argument would look like this:

Major premise:	Food products at Starbucks are standardized from one Starbucks to another.
Minor premise:	You like the pumpkin bread at one Starbucks.
Conclusion:	You will like the pumpkin bread at another Starbucks.

However, if your major premise is wrong, and the owner of one Starbucks substitutes an inferior stock of pumpkin bread, then your conclusion is wrong. Deductive reasoning is dependent upon the validity of each premise; otherwise the syllogism does not hold true. If the major premise that food products are standardized at all Starbucks' franchises does not hold true, then the argument is not valid. A good deductive argument is known as a valid argument and is such that if all its premises are true, then its conclusion must be true. Indeed, for a deductive argument to be valid, it must be absolutely impossible for both its premises to be true and its conclusion to be false.

ACTIVITY 3.3
ANALYZE THE DEDUCTIVE REASONING OF THE DECLARATION OF INDEPENDENCE

Stephen E. Lucas states that if one ignores the first introductory sentence of the Declaration, the remainder of the document forms a deductive argument. He rephrases the argument as the following:

Major premise: When government deliberately seeks to reduce the people under absolute despotism, the people have a right, indeed a duty, to alter or abolish that form of government and to create new guards for their future security.

Minor premise: The government of Great Britain has deliberately sought to reduce the American people under absolute despotism.

Conclusion: Therefore the American people have a right, indeed a duty, to abolish their present form of government and to create new guards for their future security.

Locate a copy of the complete Declaration of Independence. Identify the introduction and preamble which Lucas discussed in his article. Then identify the section of grievances against King George III which form the minor premise, and the conclusion of the Declaration which is also the conclusion of the syllogism.

INDUCTIVE REASONING

Aristotle identified another way to move logically between premises, which he called "the progress from particulars to universals." Later logicians labeled this type of logic as **inductive reasoning**. Inductive arguments are based on probability. Even if an inductive argument's premises are true, that doesn't establish with 100% certainty that their conclusions are true. Even the best inductive argument falls short of deductive validity.

These are examples of inductive reasoning:

Particular statement: Milk does not spoil as quickly if kept cold.
General statement: All perishable foods do not spoil as quickly
if kept cold.

Particular statement: Microwaves cook popcorn more quickly than
does conventional heat.
General statement: All foods cook more quickly in a microwave.

For the first example, inductive reasoning works well because cold tends to prolong the useable life of most perishable foods. The second example is more problematic. While it is true that popcorn cooks more quickly in a microwave oven, the peculiarities of microwave interaction with food molecules does not produce a uniform effect on all food stuffs. Rice, for example, does not cook much, if any, faster, than cooking on a stovetop. Also, whole eggs may explode if cooked in their shells.

A good inductive argument is known as a strong (or "cogent") inductive argument. It is such that if the premises are true, the conclusion is likely to be true.

ACTIVITY
3.4   IDENTIFY DEDUCTIVE AND INDUCTIVE REASONING

In your small group, identify an example of a deductive argument and list the premises and conclusion. Then identify an inductive argument and identify the particular statement and the general statement. Report to the class.

LOGICAL FALLACIES

Generally speaking, **logical fallacy** is an error in reasoning, as opposed to a factual error, which is simply being wrong about the facts. A deductive fallacy (sometimes called a formal fallacy) is a deductive argument that has premises that are all true, but they lead to a false conclusion, making it an invalid argument. An inductive fallacy (sometimes called an informal fallacy) appears to be an inductive argument, but the premises do not provide enough support for the conclusion to be probable. Some logical fallacies are more common than others, and, thus, have been labeled and defined. Following are a few of the most well known types:

Ad hominem (to the man) are arguments that attempt to discredit a point of view through personal attacks upon the person who has that point of view. These arguments are not relevant to the actual issue because the character of the person that holds a view says nothing about the truth of that viewpoint.

Example: Noam Chomsky is a liberal activist who opposes American intervention in other countries. Noam Chomsky's theory of transformational grammar, which suggests that humans have an innate ability to learn language, is ridiculous.

Begging the Question arguments simply assume that a point of view is true because the truth of the premise is assumed. Simply assuming a premise is true does not amount to evidence that it is true.

Example: A woman's place is in the home; therefore, women should not work.

Confusing Cause and Effect is a common problem with scientific studies in which the fact that two events are correlated implies that one causes the other.

Example: Obese people drink a lot of diet soda; therefore, diet soda causes obesity.

Post Hoc (from the Latin phrase "Post hoc, ergo proper hoc," or after this, therefore because of this) is a fallacy that concludes that one event caused another just because one occurred before the other.

Example: The Great Depression caused World War II.

Straw Man is a fallacy in which a position of an opponent is exaggerated or weakened, so that it is easier for the opponent to argue against it.

Example: Pro-choice advocates belief in murdering unborn children.

A **Slippery Slope** argument asserts that one event will inevitably lead to another event.

Example: the Dilbert cartoon below:

DILBERT: © Scott Adams/Dist. by United Feature Syndicate, Inc.

ACTIVITY 3.5

IDENTIFY LOGICAL FALLACIES

Match the following types of logical fallacies with the examples below:
Types:
Ad hominem
Begging the Question
Confusing Cause and Effect
Post Hoc

Straw Man
Slippery Slope

Examples:
1. Legalization of medical marijuana will lead to increased marijuana use by the general population.
2. Twenty-one is the best age limit for drinking because people do not mature until they are 21.
3. If you teach birth control methods, more teenage girls will get pregnant.
4. The culture wars of the 1960s were a result of parents being unable to control their children after the post-World War II baby boom.
5. Al Gore claims that global warming is a dangerous trend. Al Gore is a liberal. Therefore, there is no global warming.
6. Immigration reform advocates want to separate families and children.

**ACTIVITY
3.6**   **CREATE EXAMPLES OF LOGICAL FALLACIES**

In your small group, take the list of logical fallacies above and create an example for each of the fallacies. Each group will then report to the class one fallacy at a time, with the instructor making a list on the chalk board of the fallacies. Discuss any that are not clear cases of a particular fallacy.

ARGUMENTS FROM *PATHOS*

Pathos makes use of emotion to persuade an audience. Aristotle wrote: "Proofs from the disposition of the audience are produced whenever they are induced by the speech into an emotional state. We do not give judgment in the same way when aggrieved and when pleased, in sympathy and in revulsion."

Effective rhetors know their audiences, particularly what emotions they hold that are relevant to the issue under consideration. What motivates them? What are their fears, their hopes, their desires, and their doubts? If the audience has the same emotions as you do, fine. However, if they do not already hold those emotions, you need, through the stories you tell, the statistics you cite, and the reasoning you offer, to bring them to share the hurt, the anger, or the joy that will persuade them to share your viewpoint.

For example, when Martin Luther King, Jr., in his "I Have a Dream" speech (reprinted in Chapter 4) referred to the "hallowed spot" of the Lincoln Memorial, he was appealing to his audience's feelings of patriotism and reverence for the accomplishments of President Lincoln. Subtly, he was also garnering this emotion toward Lincoln in contemporary support of civil rights. Lincoln had issued the Emancipation Proclamation that declared all slaves to be free, yet, according to King, America had not lived up to Lincoln's promise.

READING
3.3

"PEOPLE FOR SALE"
BY E. BENJAMIN SKINNER

E. Benjamin Skinner's articles on a wide range of topics have appeared in Newsweek International, Travel and Leisure, *and other magazines. This essay was adapted from* A Crime So Monstrous: Face-to-Face with Modern-Day Slavery *and appeared in* Foreign Policy.

Most people imagine that slavery died in the 19th century. Since 1810, more than a dozen international conventions banning the slave trade have been signed. Yet today there are more slaves than at any time in human history.

And if you're going to buy one in five hours, you'd better get a move on. First, hail a taxi to JFK International Airport and hop on a direct flight to Port-au-Prince, Haiti. The flight takes three hours. After landing, take a tap-tap, a flatbed pickup retrofitted with benches and a canopy, three-quarters of the way up Route de Delmas, the capital's main street. There, on a side street, you will find a group of men standing in front of Le Réseau (the Network) barbershop. As you approach, a man steps forward: "Are you looking to get a person?"

Meet Benavil Lebhom. He smiles easily. He has a trim mustache and wears a multicolored striped golf shirt, a gold chain, and Doc Martens knockoffs. Benavil is a courtier, or broker. He holds an official real estate license and calls himself an employment agent. Two-thirds of the employees he places are child slaves. The total number of Haitian children in bondage in their own country stands at 300,000. They are restavèks, the "stay-withs," as they are euphemistically known in Creole. Forced, unpaid, they work in captivity from before dawn until night. Benavil and thousands of other formal and informal traffickers lure these children from desperately impoverished rural parents with promises of free schooling and a better life.

The negotiation to buy a child slave might sound a bit like this:

"How quickly do you think it would be possible to bring a child in? Somebody who could clean and cook?" you ask. "I don't have a very big place; I have a small apartment. But I'm wondering how much that would cost? And how quickly?"

"Three days," Benavil responds.

"And you could bring the child here?" you inquire. "Or are there children here already?"

"I don't have any here in Port-au-Prince right now," says Benavil, his eyes widening at the thought of a foreign client. "I would go out to the countryside."

You ask about additional expenses. "Would I have to pay for transportation?"

"Bon," says Benavil. "A hundred U.S."

Smelling a rip-off, you press him, "And that's just for transportation?"

"Transportation would be about 100 Haitian," says Benavil, "because you'd have to get out there. Plus, [hotel and] food on the trip. Five hundred gourdes"—around $13.

"OK, 500 Haitian," you say.

Now you ask the big question: "And what would your fee be?" Benavil's eyes narrow as he determines how much he can take you for.

"A hundred. American."

"That seems like a lot," you say, with a smile so as not to kill the deal. "Could you bring down your fee to 50 U.S.?"

Benavil pauses. But only for effect. He knows he's still got you for much more than a Haitian would pay. "Oui," he says with a smile.

But the deal isn't done. Benavil leans in close. "This is a rather delicate question. Is this someone you want as just a worker? Or also someone who will be a 'partner'? You understand what I mean?"

You don't blink at being asked if you want the child for sex. "Is it possible to have someone who could be both?"

"Oui!" Benavil responds enthusiastically.

If you're interested in taking your purchase back to the United States, Benavil tells you that he can "arrange" the proper papers to make it look as though you've adopted the child.

He offers you a 13-year-old girl.

"That's a little bit old," you say.

"I know of another girl who's 12. Then ones that are 10, 11," he responds.

The negotiation is finished, and you tell Benavil not to make any moves without further word from you. You have successfully arranged to buy a human being for 50 bucks.

It would be nice if that conversation were fictional. It is not. I recorded it in October 2005 as part of four years of research into slavery on five continents. In the popular consciousness, "slavery" has come to be little more than just a metaphor for undue hardship. Investment bankers routinely refer to themselves as "high-paid wage slaves." Human rights activists may call $1-an-hour sweatshop laborers slaves, regardless of the fact that they are paid and can often walk away from the job.

The reality of slavery is far different. Slavery exists today on an unprecedented scale. In Africa, tens of thousands are chattel slaves, seized in war or tucked away for generations. Across Europe, Asia, and the Americas, traffickers have forced as many as 2 million into prostitution or labor. In South Asia, which has the highest concentration of slaves on the planet, nearly 10 million languish in bondage, unable to leave their captors until they pay off "debts," legal fictions that in many cases are generations old.

Few in the developed world have a grasp of the enormity of modern-day slavery. Fewer still are doing anything to combat it.... Between 2000 and 2006, the U.S. Justice Department increased human trafficking prosecutions from 3 to 32, and convictions from 10 to 98. By the end of 2006, 27 states had passed anti-trafficking laws. Yet, during the same period, the United States liberated only about 2 percent of its own modern-day slaves. As many as 17,500 new slaves continue to enter bondage in the United States every year...Many feel that sex slavery is particularly revolting—and it is. I saw it firsthand. In a Bucharest brothel, I was offered a mentally handicapped suicidal girl in exchange for a used car. But for every woman or child enslaved in commercial sex, there are some 15 men, women, and children enslaved in other fields, such as domestic work or agricultural labor.

Save for the fact that he is male, Gonoo Lal Kol typifies the average slave of our modern age. (At his request, I have changed his name.) Like a majority of the world's slaves, Gonoo is in debt bondage in South Asia. In his case, in an Indian quarry. Like most slaves, Gonoo is illiterate and unaware of the Indian laws that ban his bondage and provide for sanctions against his master. His story, told to me near his four-foot-high stone and grass hutch, represents the other side of the "Indian Miracle."

Gonoo lives in Lohagara Dhal, a forgotten corner of Uttar Pradesh, a north Indian state that contains 8 percent of the world's poor. I met him one evening in December 2005 as he walked with two dozen other laborers in tattered and filthy clothes. Behind them was the quarry. In that pit, Gonoo, a member of the historically outcast Kol tribe, worked with his family 14 hours a day. His tools were a hammer and a pike. His hands were covered in calluses, his fingertips worn away.

Gonoo's master is a tall, stout, surly contractor named Ramesh Garg. He makes his money by enslaving entire families forced to work for no pay beyond alcohol, grain, and subsistence expenses. Slavery scholar Kevin Bales estimates that a slave in the 19th-century American South had to work 20 years to recoup his or her purchase price. Gonoo and the other slaves earn a profit for Garg in two years.

Every single man, woman, and child in Lohagara Dhal is a slave. But, in theory at least, Garg neither bought nor owns them. The seed of Gonoo's slavery, for instance, was a loan of 62 cents. In 1958 his grandfather borrowed that amount from the owner of a farm where he worked. Three generations and three slave masters later, Gonoo's family remains in bondage.

Recently, many bold, underfunded groups have taken up the challenge of tearing out the roots of slavery. Some gained fame through dramatic slave rescues. Most learned that freeing slaves is impossible unless the slaves themselves choose to be free. Among the Kol of Uttar Pradesh, for instance, an organization called Pragati Gramodyog Sansthan (PGS)—the Progressive Institute for Village Enterprises—has helped hundreds of families break the grip of the quarry contractors.

The psychological, social, and economic bonds of slavery run deep, and for governments to be truly effective in eradicating slavery, they must partner with groups that can offer slaves a way to pull themselves up from bondage. One way to do that is to replicate the work of grassroots organizations such as the India-based MSEMVS (Society for Human Development and Women's Empowerment). In 1996 the group launched free transitional schools where children who had been enslaved learned skills and acquired enough literacy to move on to formal schooling. The group also targeted mothers, providing them with training and start-up materials for microenterprises....In recent years, the United States has shown an increasing willingness to help fund these kinds of organizations, one encouraging sign that the message may be getting through.

For four years, I encountered dozens of enslaved people, several of whom traffickers like Benavil actually offered to sell to me. I did not pay for a human life anywhere. And, with one exception, I always withheld action to save any one person, in the hope that my research would later help to save many more. At times, that still feels like an excuse for cowardice. But the hard work of real emancipation can't be the burden of a select few. For thousands of slaves, grassroots groups like PGS and MSEMVS can help bring freedom. Until governments define slavery in appropriately concise terms, prosecute the crime aggressively in all its forms, and encourage groups that empower slaves to free themselves, however, millions more will remain in bondage. And our collective promise of abolition will continue to mean nothing at all.

**ACTIVITY
3.7**   **ANALYZE AN ARGUMENT FROM *PATHOS***

1. After reading Skinner's essay on slavery, reread the part that narrates him negotiating to buy a child slave. Then freewrite for five minutes about how that negotiation made you feel.

2. Most people feel emotional when they read about a child in distress, and Skinner further highlights that emotional effect by putting this particular episode in dialog, always a point of emphasis in an essay. Do you think Skinner deliberately appealed to pathos in this part of his essay? Discuss in your group.

3. List other areas where the essay evokes an emotional response. Consider why, and freewrite on your feelings and beliefs that are brought into play. How did the author know that you would probably react this way?

4. Although much of Skinner's argument relies on pathos, he also provides statistics and references to authorities to bolster his argument. Identify the paragraphs which provide statistics or other evidence that would qualify as logos.

ARGUMENTS FROM *ETHOS*

No exact translation exists in English for the word ethos, but it can be loosely translated as the credibility of the speaker. This credibility generates good will which colors all the arguments, examples, and quotes the rhetor utilizes in his text. Rhetors can enhance their credibility by evidence of intelligence, virtue, and goodwill and diminish it by seeming petty, dishonest, and mean-spirited. In addition, a speaker or writer can enhance his or her own credibility by references to quotes or the actions of authorities or leaders.

Aristotle wrote: Proofs from character [*ethos*] are produced, whenever the speech is given in such a way as to render the speaker worthy of credence—we more readily and sooner believe reasonable men on all matters in general and absolutely on questions where precision is impossible and two views can be maintained.

For example, Martin Luther King, Jr., pointed out in his "I Have a Dream" speech, that, according to the framers of the Constitution and the Declaration of Independence, "unalienable Rights" of "Life, Liberty and the pursuit of Happiness" apply equally to black men and white men. He was, in effect, borrowing the *ethos* of Thomas Jefferson and the framers of the Constitution in support of the unalienable rights of blacks.

READING
3.4   "A WOMAN CAN LEARN ANYTHING A MAN CAN"
                              BY CAROLYN TURK

Carolyn Turk's essay was a "My Turn" essay in Newsweek. *The magazine each week prints an essay written by someone who is not a professional writer but who has a story to tell. Turk, as she says in her essay, is a mechanical engineer.*

When I was a kid, everything in my bedroom was pink. I have two sisters and we had a complete miniature kitchen, a herd of My Little Ponies and several Barbie and Ken dolls. We didn't have any toy trucks, G.I. Joes or basketballs. We did have a Wiffle ball set, but you would have been hard-pressed to find it in our playroom. Tomboys we weren't.

So some people may find it ironic that I grew up to be a mechanical engineer. In fact, I am the only female engineer at my company. In order to get my college degree, I had to take a lot of math and science classes. I also had to work with a team of students as part of a national competition to convert a gas-guzzling SUV into a hybrid electric vehicle—that's where I learned how to fix cars. I'm proud to say that I got A's in all my classes, including multivariable calculus and differential equations. I've always been pretty good at math and design, but I didn't understand where that could take me. I was expected to go to college, but no one ever told me I'd make a good engineer someday.

When I was in high school, I didn't know the first thing about engineering. I couldn't have distinguished a transmission from an alternator. The car I drove needed some work but I was afraid to take it to the mechanic. Because honestly, the mechanic could have shown me an electric can opener and said, "This is part of your car and it's broken—pay me to fix it," and I wouldn't have known any better.

At the end of my junior year of high school, I heard about a summer program designed to interest girls in engineering. The six-week program was free, and students were given college credit and a dorm room at the University of Maryland. I applied to the program, not because I wanted to be an engineer, but because I was craving independence and wanted to get out of my parents' house for six weeks. I was accepted to the program and I earned six engineering credits. The next year I entered the university as an engineering major. Five years later I had a degree and three decent job offers.

I can't help shuddering when I hear about studies that show that women are at a disadvantage when it comes to math. They imply that I am somehow abnormal. I'm not, but I do know that if I hadn't stumbled into that summer program, I wouldn't be an engineer.

When I was growing up I was told, as many students are, to do what I am best at. But I didn't know what that was. Most people think that when you are good at something, it comes easily to you. But this is what I discovered: just because a subject is difficult to learn, it does not mean you are not good at it. You just have to grit your teeth and work harder to get good at it. Once you do, there's a strong chance you will enjoy it more than anything else.

In eighth grade I took algebra. On one test I got only 36 percent of the answers correct. I failed the next one, too. I started to think, Maybe I'm just no good at this. I was lucky enough to have a teacher who didn't take my bad grades as a judgment of my abilities, but simply as an indication that I should study more. He pulled me aside and told me he knew I could do better. He let me retake the tests, and I pulled my grade up to an A.

I studied a lot in college, too. I had moments of panic while sitting underneath the buzzing fluorescent lights in the engineering library on Saturday afternoons, when I worried that the estrogen in my body was preventing me from understanding thermodynamics. But the guys in my classes had to work just as hard, and I knew that I couldn't afford to lose confidence in myself. I didn't want to choose between my femininity and a good career. So I reminded myself that those studies, the ones that say that math comes more naturally to men, are based on a faulty premise: that you can judge a person's abilities separate from the cultural cues that she has received since she was an infant. No man is an island. No woman is, either.

Why are we so quick to limit ourselves? I'm not denying that most little girls love dolls and most little boys love videogames, and it may be true that some people favor the right side of their brain, and others the left. But how relevant is that to me, or to anyone, as an individual? Instead of translating our differences into hard and fast conclusions about the human brain, why can't we focus instead on how incredibly flexible we are? Instead of using what we know as a reason why women can't learn physics, maybe we should consider the possibility that our brains are more powerful than we imagine.

Here's a secret: math and science don't come easily to most people. No one was ever born knowing calculus. A woman can learn anything a man can, but first she needs to know that she can do it, and that takes a leap of faith. It also helps to have selective hearing.

**ACTIVITY
3.8** **ANALYZING AN ARGUMENT FROM *ETHOS***

1. In the previous reading, Carolyn Turk draws upon the ethos of her success as an engineering major and as a mechanical engineer to provide evidence that women can do what men can do. In your group, discuss how Turk's demonstrated success in what is typically thought of as a man's field, engineering, increases her credibility.

2. How do you think this essay would stand up against essays by men or women with more credentials who argue against her opinion that women can do anything men can do? What kinds of other evidence could Turk have offered that would strengthen her argument?

3. Is Turk appealing to pathos when she says she had "moments of panic"? What is she referring to when she uses this phrase and what effect do you

think she wants to have on her audience by using the phrase?

4. Turk presents a logical argument that she is well suited to her engineering profession. Summarize her logical argument.

COMBINING *ETHOS, PATHOS,* AND *LOGOS*

Did you notice that the triangle earlier in this chapter representing Aristotle's three appeals is equilateral, meaning that all sides are equal in length. This is to illustrate that the *ethos, pathos,* and *logos* elements are equally important and merit equal attention in the writing process. No text is purely based on one of the three appeals, though more of the argument in a particular text may be based on one appeal rather than another. In each writing situation, however, an effective rhetor will think about how each plays into the structure of the argument.

In today's world, for example, a public speaker's effectiveness is affected by the ability to use a teleprompter, or, if one is not available, to memorize a speech well enough so he or she has to refer to notes infrequently. If a speaker's eyes flit from left to right across the text of a teleprompter, it shows on television, and reduces the credibility, or ethos of the speaker, no matter how well the other appeals are executed in the speech. The equivalent of presentation for a written text would be to produce a document that is essentially free from surface grammatical errors, is spell-checked, and is printed on good paper stock with the correct margins and type size. If the document does not look professional, it will lose credibility or ethos no matter what it says.

To give another example, E. Benjamin Skinner's essay "People for Sale" relies on the highly emotional image of a child being sold into slavery for its major appeal. However, if you read back through the essay, you will see that it has a clear thesis, which could be stated as the following: slavery exists in the present time, even in the United States, and it is not even that difficult to buy a slave. The essay is well organized and offers a variety of evidence, including statistics and first-person observation. Logos may not stand out as the primary appeal in Skinner's essay, but it is nevertheless strong in its appeal to *logos*.

If you want to develop your writing skills, it is essential that you pay attention to each of Aristotle's appeals—*ethos, pathos,* and *logos*.

**ACTIVITY
3.9**   **WRITING ABOUT *ETHOS, PATHOS,* AND *LOGOS***

Choose one of the texts in Chapters 1, 2, or 3 and write an essay that identifies the *ethos, pathos,* and *logos* of the particular text and then discuss how the three appeals together are used by the author to produce an effective essay. Alternatively, discuss which of the appeals is weak in the particular essay and how that affects the effectiveness of the essay.

NOTES to "The Stylistic Artistry of the Declaration of Independence"
© 1989 by Stephen E. Lucas

(1) Moses Coit Tyler, *The Literary History of the American Revolution* (1897), vol. 1, p. 520. The best known study of the style of the Declaration is Carl Becker's "The Literary Qualities of the Declaration," in his *The Declaration of Independence: A Study in the History of Political Ideas* (1922), pp. 194-223. Useful also are Robert Ginsberg, "The Declaration as Rhetoric," in Robert Ginsberg, ed., *A Casebook on the Declaration of Independence* (1967), pp. 219-244; Edwin Gittleman, "Jefferson's 'Slave Narrative': The Declaration of Independence as a Literary Text," *Early American Literature* 8 (1974): 239-256; and James Boyd White, *When Words Lose Their Meaning: Constitutions and Reconstitutions of Language, Character, and Community* (1984), 231-240. Although most books on the Declaration contain a chapter on the "style" of the document, those chapters are typically historical accounts of the evolution of the text from its drafting by Thomas Jefferson through its approval by the Continental Congress or philosophical speculations about the meaning of its famous passages.

(2) As Garry Wills demonstrates in *Inventing America: Jefferson's Declaration of Independence* (1978), there are two Declarations of Independence the version drafted by Thomas Jefferson and that revised and adopted on July 4, 1776, by the Continental Congress sitting as a committee of the whole. Altogether Congress deleted 630 words from Jefferson's draft and added 146, producing a final text of 1,322 words (excluding the title). Although Jefferson complained that Congress "mangled" his manuscript and altered it "much for the worse," the judgment of posterity, stated well by Becker, is that "Congress left the Declaration better than it found it" (*Declaration of Independence*, p. 209). In any event, for better or worse, it was Congress's text that presented America's case to the world, and it is that text with which we are concerned in this essay.

(3) Nothing in this essay should be interpreted to mean that a firm line can be drawn between style and substance in the Declaration or in any other work of political or literary discourse. As Peter Gay has noted, style is "form and content woven into the texture of every art and craft. . . . Apart from a few mechanical tricks of rhetoric, manner is indissolubly linked to matter; style shapes and is in turn shaped by, substance" (*Style in History* [1974], p. 3).

(4) All quotations from the Declaration follow the text as presented in Julian P. Boyd et al., eds., *The Papers of Thomas Jefferson* (1950), vol. 1, pp. 429-432.

(5) Ephraim Chambers, *Cyclopedia: Or, An Universal Dictionary of Arts and Sciences* (1728), vol. 2, p. 621; Jonathan Edwards, *Freedom of the Will,* ed. Paul Ramsey (1957), p. 149.

(6) Declaration of the Lords and Commons to Justify Their Taking Up Arms, August 1642, in John Rushworth, ed., *Historical Collections of Private Passages of State, Weighty Matters in Law, Remarkable Proceedings in Five Parliaments* (1680-1722), vol. 4, pp. 761-768; Declaration of the Continental Congress Setting Forth the Causes and Necessity of Their Taking Up Arms, July 1775, in James H. Hutson, ed., *A Decent Respect to the Opinions of Mankind: Congressional State Papers, 1774-1776* (1975), pp. 89-98. The importance of necessity as a justification for war among nations is evident in the many declarations of war issued by European monarchs throughout the seventeenth and eighteenth centuries and is discussed in Tavers Twiss, *The Law of Nations Considered as Independent Political Communities* (1863), pp. 54-55.

(7) The first additional invocation of the doctrine of necessity in the Declaration comes immediately after the preamble, when Congress states, "Such has been the patient sufferance of these Colonies; and such is now the necessity which constrains them to alter their former systems of Government." The second is at the end of the penultimate section, in which Congress ends its denunciation of the British people by announcing, "We must, therefore, acquiesce in the necessity, which denounces our Separation, and hold them, as we hold the rest of mankind, Enemies in War, in Peace Friends."

(8) [Thomas Paine], *Common Sense: Addressed to the Inhabitants of America . . .* (1776), pp. 41, 43.

(9) Samuel Adams to Joseph Hawley, Apr. 15, 1776, *Letters of Delegates to Congress, 1774-1789*, ed. Paul H. Smith (1976), vol. 3, p. 528; Thomas Jefferson, Notes of Proceedings in the Continental Congress, Jefferson Papers 1: 312.

(10) Jonathan Mayhew, *A Discourse Concerning Unlimited Submission and Nonresistance to the Higher Powers . . .* (1750), p. 45; [John, Lord Somers], *The Judgment of Whole Kingdoms and Nations, Concerning the Rights, Power and Prerogative of Kings, and the Rights, Privileges and Properties of the People* (1710), par. 186; Algernon Sidney, *Discourses Concerning Government* (1693), p. 181; John Hoadly, ed., *The Works of Benjamin Hoadly* (1773), vol. 2, p. 36; "Pacificus," *Pennsylvania Gazette*, Sept. 14, 1774.

(11) Becker, *Declaration of Independence*, p. 201. (12) Hugh Blair, *Lectures on Rhetoric and Belles Lettres* (1783), vol. 1, pp. 206-207, 259.

(13) "Thoughts on English Prosody" was enclosed in an undated letter of ca. October 1786 to the Marquis de Chastellux. The letter is printed in Jefferson Papers 10: 498; the draft of Jefferson's essay, which has not been printed, is with the letter to Chastellux in the Thomas Jefferson Papers, Library of Congress, Washington, DC. Julian P. Boyd, "The Declaration of Independence: The Mystery of the Lost Original," *Pennsylvania Magazine of History and Biography*

100 (1976): 455-462, discusses "Thoughts on English Prosody" and its relation to Jefferson's reading text of the Declaration. Given the changes made by Congress in some sections of the Declaration, it should be noted that the style of the preamble is distinctly Jeffersonian and was approved by Congress with only two minor changes in wording from Jefferson's fair copy as reported by the Committee of Five.

(14) Jefferson to Henry Lee, May 5, 1825, *The Writings of Thomas Jefferson*, ed. Paul Leicester Ford (1892-1899), vol. 10, p. 343.

(15) Wilbur Samuel Howell, "The Declaration of Independence and Eighteenth-Century Logic," *William and Mary Quarterly,* 3d Ser. 18 (1961): 463-484, claims Jefferson consciously structured the Declaration as a syllogism with a self-evident major premise to fit the standards for scientific proof advanced in William Duncan's *Elements of Logick*, a leading logical treatise of the eighteenth century. As I argue in a forthcoming essay, however, there is no hard evidence to connect Duncan's book with the Declaration. Jefferson may have read *Elements of Logick* while he was a student at the College of William and Mary, but we are not certain that he did. He owned a copy of it, but we cannot establish whether the edition he owned was purchased before or after 1776. We cannot even say with complete confidence that Jefferson inserted the words "self-evident" in the Declaration; if he did, it was only as an afterthought in the process of polishing his original draft. Moreover, upon close examination it becomes clear that the Declaration does not fit the method of scientific reasoning recommended in Duncan's *Logick.* Its "self- evident" truths are not self-evident in the rigorous technical sense used by Duncan; it does not provide the definitions of terms that Duncan regards as the crucial first step in syllogistic demonstration; and it does not follow Duncan's injunction that both the minor premise and the major premise must be self-evident if a conclusion is to be demonstrated in a single act of reasoning. The syllogism had been part of the intellectual baggage of Western civilization for two thousand years, and the notion of self-evident truth was central to eighteenth-century philosophy. Jefferson could readily have used both without turning to Duncan's *Logick* for instruction.

FINDING THE KAIROS OF THE ARGUMENT

Each time a rhetor (a writer or speaker) constructs an argument, he or she is working within a context of a certain moment, a particular time and place. This moment, which the ancient Greeks called **kairos** (a word which has no exact English translation) may include audience and culture in addition to time and place. Kairos both constrains and enables what a rhetor can say or write effectively in a context. For example, when Martin Luther King, Jr., gave his "I Have a Dream Speech," his words were carefully crafted to take into consideration the setting in front of the Lincoln Memorial. He said, "Five score years ago, a great American, in whose symbolic shadow we stand today, signed the Emancipation Proclamation." The words "five score" recall the "four score and seven years ago" of Lincoln's words in the Gettysburg Address. And King also pointed out that he and his audience that day stood in the "symbolic shadow" of Lincoln who signed the Emancipation Proclamation. In these ways, he made use of Lincoln's shadow to legitimize what he was saying about civil rights.

In other ways, however, the kairos of the moment limited what he could say. His audience included both the thousands of people in front of him who were dedicated to the cause of racial equality and also the audience of those millions watching on television who may or may not have agreed with his message. Thus, the tone of his message needed to be subtly measured not to antagonize those among his audience, particularly the television audience, who may have opposed aspects of the civil rights movement such as school integration. However, he spoke to let both his supporters and his opponents know, "The whirlwinds of revolt will continue to shake the foundations of our nation until the bright day of justice emerges." Yes, King advocated non-violent demonstrations, but they were demonstrations none-theless; he was putting opponents on notice that the disruptions caused by demonstrations would continue "until justice emerges." King consistently took the high road, while maintaining the power of the kairotic moment when he spoke, one reason that his words continue to be studied decades after his death.

READING 4.1

"I Have a Dream" by Martin Luther King, Jr.

Martin Luther King, Jr., delivered this speech August 28, 1963, at the Lincoln Memorial in Washington, D.C. as part of the March on Washington for Jobs and Freedom. A Baptist minister, King received the Nobel Peace Prize in 1964 for his efforts to end racial discrimination through non-violent means. He was assassinated in 1968.

I am happy to join with you today in what will go down in history as the greatest demonstration for freedom in the history of our nation.

Five score years ago, a great American, in whose symbolic shadow we stand today, signed the Emancipation Proclamation. This momentous decree came as a great beacon light of hope to millions of Negro slaves who had been seared in the flames of withering injustice. It came as a joyous daybreak to end the long night of their captivity.

But one hundred years later, the Negro still is not free. One hundred years later, the life of the Negro is still sadly crippled by the manacles of segregation and the chains of discrimination. One hundred years later, the Negro lives on a lonely island of poverty in the midst of a vast ocean of material prosperity. One hundred years later, the Negro is still languished in the corners of American society and finds himself an exile in his own land. And so we've come here today to dramatize a shameful condition.

In a sense we've come to our nation's capital to cash a check. When the architects of our republic wrote the magnificent words of the Constitution and the Declaration of Independence, they were signing a promissory note to which every American was to fall heir. This note was a promise that all men, yes, black men as well as white men, would be guaranteed the "unalienable Rights" of "Life, Liberty and the pursuit of Happiness." It is obvious today that America has defaulted on this promissory note, insofar as her citizens of color are concerned. Instead of honoring this sacred obligation, America has given the Negro people a bad check, a check which has come back marked "insufficient funds."

But we refuse to believe that the bank of justice is bankrupt. We refuse to believe that there are insufficient funds in the great vaults of opportunity of this nation. And so, we've come to cash this check, a check that will give us upon demand the riches of freedom and the security of justice.

We have also come to this hallowed spot to remind America of the fierce urgency of Now. This is no time to engage in the luxury of cooling off or to take the tranquilizing drug of gradualism. Now is the time to make real the promises of democracy. Now is the time to rise from the dark and desolate valley of segregation to the sunlit path of racial justice. Now is the time to lift our nation from the quicksands of racial injustice to the solid rock of brotherhood. Now is the time to make justice a reality for all of God's children.

It would be fatal for the nation to overlook the urgency of the moment. This sweltering summer of the Negro's legitimate discontent will not pass until there is an invigorating autumn of freedom and equality. Nineteen sixty-three is not an end, but a beginning. And those who hope that the Negro needed to blow off steam and will now be content will have a rude awakening if the nation returns to business as usual. And there will be neither rest nor tranquility in America until the Negro is granted his citizenship rights. The whirlwinds of revolt will continue to shake the foundations of our nation until the bright day of justice emerges.

But there is something that I must say to my people, who stand on the warm threshold which leads into the palace of justice: In the process of gaining our rightful place, we must not be guilty of wrongful deeds. Let us not seek to satisfy our thirst for freedom by drinking from the cup of bitterness and hatred. We must forever conduct our struggle on the high plane of dignity and discipline. We must not allow our creative protest to degenerate into physical violence. Again and again, we must rise to the majestic heights of meeting physical force with soul force.

The marvelous new militancy which has engulfed the Negro community must not lead us to a distrust of all white people, for many of our white brothers, as evidenced by their presence here today, have come to realize that their destiny is tied up with our destiny. And they have come to realize that their freedom is inextricably bound to our freedom.

> We cannot walk alone.

> And as we walk, we must make the pledge that we shall always march ahead.

> We cannot turn back.

There are those who are asking the devotees of civil rights, "When will you be satisfied?" We can never be satisfied as long as the Negro is the victim of the unspeakable horrors of police brutality. We can never be satisfied as long as our bodies, heavy with the fatigue of travel, cannot gain lodging in the motels of the highways and the hotels of the cities. We cannot be satisfied as long as the negro's basic mobility is from a smaller ghetto to a larger one. We can never be satisfied as long as our children are stripped of their self-hood and robbed of their dignity by a sign stating: "For Whites Only." We cannot be satisfied as long as a Negro in Mississippi cannot vote and a Negro in New York believes he has nothing for which to vote. No, no, we are not satisfied, and we will not be satisfied until "justice rolls down like waters, and righteousness like a mighty stream."[1]

I am not unmindful that some of you have come here out of great trials and tribulations. Some of you have come fresh from narrow jail cells. And some of you have come from areas where your quest— quest for freedom left you battered by the storms of persecution and staggered by the winds of police brutality. You have been the veterans of creative suffering. Continue to work with the faith that unearned suffering is redemptive. Go back to Mississippi, go back to Alabama, go back to South Carolina, go back to Georgia, go back to Louisiana, go back to the slums and ghettos of our northern cities, knowing that somehow this situation can and will be changed.

Let us not wallow in the valley of despair, I say to you today, my friends.

And so even though we face the difficulties of today and tomorrow, I still have a dream. It is a dream deeply rooted in the American dream.

I have a dream that one day this nation will rise up and live out the true meaning of its creed: "We hold these truths to be self-evident, that all men are created equal."

I have a dream that one day on the red hills of Georgia, the sons of former slaves and the sons of former slave owners will be able to sit down together at the table of brotherhood.

I have a dream that one day even the state of Mississippi, a state sweltering with the heat of injustice, sweltering with the heat of oppression, will be transformed into an oasis of freedom and justice.

I have a dream that my four little children will one day live in a nation where they will not be judged by the color of their skin but by the content of their character.

I have a dream today!

I have a dream that one day, down in Alabama, with its vicious racists, with its governor having his lips dripping with the words of "interposition" and "nullification"—one day right there in Alabama little black boys and black girls will be able to join hands with little white boys and white girls as sisters and brothers.

I have a dream today!

I have a dream that one day every valley shall be exalted, and every hill and mountain shall be made low, the rough places will be made plain, and the crooked places will be made straight; "and the glory of the Lord shall be revealed and all flesh shall see it together."[2]

This is our hope, and this is the faith that I go back to the South with.

With this faith, we will be able to hew out of the mountain of despair a stone of hope. With this faith, we will be able to transform the jangling discords of our nation into a beautiful symphony of brotherhood. With this faith, we will be able to work together, to pray together, to struggle together, to go to jail together, to stand up for freedom together, knowing that we will be free one day.

And this will be the day—this will be the day when all of God's children will be able to sing with new meaning:

>My country 'tis of thee, sweet land of liberty, of thee I sing.
>Land where my fathers died, land of the Pilgrim's pride,
>From every mountainside, let freedom <u>ring</u>!

>And if America is to be a great nation, this must become true.

>And so let freedom ring from the prodigious hilltops of New Hampshire.
>Let freedom ring from the mighty mountains of New York.
>Let freedom ring from the heightening Alleghenies of Pennsylvania.
>Let freedom ring from the snow-capped Rockies of Colorado.
>Let freedom ring from the curvaceous slopes of California.

>But not only that:
>Let freedom ring from Stone Mountain of Georgia.
>Let freedom ring from Lookout Mountain of Tennessee.
>Let freedom ring from every hill and molehill of Mississippi.
>From every mountainside, let freedom ring.

And when this happens, when we allow freedom to ring, when we let it ring from every village and every hamlet, from every state and every city, we will be able to speed up that day when all of God's children, black men and white men, Jews and Gentiles, Protestants and Catholics, will be able to join hands and sing in the words of the old Negro spiritual:

Free at last! Free at last!

Thank God Almighty, we are free at last![3]

[1] Amos 5:24 (rendered precisely in The American Standard Version of the Holy Bible)

[2] Isaiah 40:4-5 (King James Version of the Holy Bible). Quotation marks are excluded from part of this moment in the text because King's rendering of Isaiah 40:4 does not precisely follow the KJV version from which he quotes (e.g., "hill" and "mountain" are reversed in the KJV). King's rendering of Isaiah 40:5, however, is precisely quoted from the KJV.

[3] "Free at Last" from *American Negro Songs* by J.W. Work.

ACTIVITY 4.1

USE MICROSOFT'S COMMENT FEATURE TO ANNOTATE A TEXT

If you download Dr. Martin Luther King's speech from AmericanRhetoric.com, you can make use of Microsoft's Comment feature to annotate the speech with your comments, as is done in the example below. In Microsoft Word, highlight the text you want to annotate, go to the "Insert" pull-down menu and select "Comment." A box will appear where you can enter your comment.

I am happy to join with you today in what will go down in history as the greatest demonstration for freedom in the history of our nation.

Five score years ago, a great American, in whose symbolic shadow we stand today, signed the Emancipation Proclamation. This momentous decree came as a great beacon light of hope to millions of Negro slaves who had been seared in the flames of withering injustice. It came as a joyous daybreak to end the long night of their captivity.

> 2/7/09 12:38 AM
> **Comment:** Reference to Lincoln's Gettysburg Address

But one hundred years later, the Negro still is not free. One hundred years later, the life of the Negro is still sadly crippled by the manacles of segregation and the chains of discrimination. One hundred years later, the Negro lives on a lonely island of poverty in the midst of a vast ocean of material prosperity. One hundred years later, the Negro is

ACTIVITY 4.2

DISCUSS "I HAVE A DREAM"

Read the "I Have a Dream" speech by Rev. Martin Luther King, Jr., and, if possible, watch the speech. It is archived at http://www.americanrhetoric.com, where it is listed as the most requested speech and #1 in their list of the top 100 American speeches.

1. Discuss the kairos of Dr. King's speech. What was the occasion? Who was his audience, both present and absent? What were the issues he spoke about?
2. How did Dr. King take advantage of the kairos of the situation in the wording of his speech?
3. Why do you think the speech continues to be so popular and influential?

CONSIDER THE ELEMENTS OF KAIROS

Not every speech is given in front of the Lincoln Memorial, but every speech or written text has a kairos, and the effective rhetor takes advantage of factors relating to the audience and the situation which could not happen just any time and any place. Following are some suggestions for maximizing the advantages of kairos.

- *Determine the kairotic moment.* What is the timeliness of the issue? Has something happened recently regarding this issue that can be emphasized in an argument? For example, if you are writing about the death penalty, focusing upon a recent case or a recent protest would emphasize the timeliness of the issue.

- *Know your audience.* What are the characteristics of the audience? Do they agree with your position on the issue or not? What is their educational level and extent of their knowledge about the subject? For example, if you are writing about immigration policy reform, does your audience believe there is a need for reform? Do they have personal experience with illegal or legal immigrants? You can judge the amount of background information you need to provide based upon the characteristics of your audience. Also, the most important members of the audience, so far as an argument is concerned, are not those who already agree with you but those who are neutral or even slightly opposed to your position but willing to listen. As King did, be careful not to phrase your argument in ways that are insulting to people who do not agree with you, for if you do so, they will stop listening to you.

- *Establish your personal ethos.* As a rhetor, do you have a personal connection to the topic? For example, if you are writing about the pros and cons of using medication to treat ADHD, do you yourself have that condition or know intimately someone who does? If so, it may be appropriate to include a mention of your story, along with other background information in your essay. If you have no personal connection to your topic, find the stories of others that do have such a connection and become their advocate.

- *Find ground to stand on.* This may not work for every essay, but is there something about the place where you stand, literally or figuratively, that adds ethos to your argument, as Martin Luther King stood at the Lincoln Memorial? If, for example, you live in a border community, you stand at an important juncture for issues such as immigration, free-trade, and national security. In the essay that follows, "How Clean, Green Atomic Energy Can Stop Global Warming," the authors begin with the sentence, "On a cool spring morning a quarter century ago, a place in Pennsylvania called Three Mile Island..." Thus, they place themselves figuratively at that critical place in the atomic energy debate—Three Mile Island.

ACTIVITY
4.3
IDENTIFY AUDIENCES

Consider three different types of readings in Chapter 1 and 2—Jet Blue's
Passenger Bill of Rights, the essay "Smokers Get a Raw Deal," and President-
Elect Obama's victory speech." Who is the audience in each case? How
does each make use of kairos to address the needs and interests of the audiences?

READING
4.2

"HOW CLEAN, GREEN ATOMIC ENERGY
CAN STOP GLOBAL WARMING"
BY PETER SCHWARTZ AND SPENCER REISS

In this essay, originally published in Wired *in 2005, Peter Schwartz
and Spencer Reiss argue that, because of global warming and
the energy crisis, it is time to take another look at nuclear energy.
Schwartz is the author of* The Foreign Policy of Self-Interest: A
Moral Ideal for America *and Reiss has been a contributing editor
for* Wired.

On a cool spring morning a quarter century ago, a place in
Pennsylvania called Three Mile Island exploded into the headlines
and stopped the US nuclear power industry in its tracks. What had
been billed as the clean, cheap, limitless energy source for a shining
future was suddenly too hot to handle.

In the years since, we've searched for alternatives, pouring
billions of dollars into windmills, solar panels, and biofuels. We've
designed fantastically efficient lightbulbs, air conditioners, and
refrigerators. We've built enough gas-fired generators to bankrupt
California. But mainly, each year we hack 400 million more tons of
coal out of Earth's crust than we did a quarter century before, light it
on fire, and shoot the proceeds into the atmosphere.

The consequences aren't pretty. Burning coal and other fossil fuels is driving climate change, which is blamed for everything
from western forest fires and Florida hurricanes to melting polar ice

sheets and flooded Himalayan hamlets. On top of that, coal-burning electric power plants have fouled the air with enough heavy metals and other noxious pollutants to cause 15,000 premature deaths annually in the US alone, according to a Harvard School of Public Health study. Believe it or not, a coal-fired plant releases 100 times more radioactive material than an equivalent nuclear reactor—right into the air, too, not into some carefully guarded storage site. (And, by the way, more than 5,200 Chinese coal miners perished in accidents last year.)

Burning hydrocarbons is a luxury that a planet with 6 billion energy-hungry souls can't afford. There's only one sane, practical alternative: nuclear power.

We now know that the risks of splitting atoms pale beside the dreadful toll exacted by fossil fuels. Radiation containment, waste disposal, and nuclear weapons proliferation are manageable problems in a way that global warming is not. Unlike the usual green alternatives—water, wind, solar, and biomass—nuclear energy is here, now, in industrial quantities. Sure, nuke plants are expensive to build— upward of $2 billion apiece—but they start to look cheap when you factor in the true cost to people and the planet of burning fossil fuels. And nuclear is our best hope for cleanly and efficiently generating hydrogen, which would end our other ugly hydrocarbon addiction— dependence on gasoline and diesel for transport.

Some of the world's most thoughtful greens have discovered the logic of nuclear power, including Gaia theorist James Lovelock, Greenpeace cofounder Patrick Moore, and Britain's Bishop Hugh Montefiore, a longtime board member of Friends of the Earth. Western Europe is quietly backing away from planned nuclear phaseouts. Finland has ordered a big reactor specifically to meet the terms of the Kyoto Protocol on climate change. China's new nuke plants—26 by 2025—are part of a desperate effort at smog control.

Even the shell-shocked US nuclear industry is coming out of its stupor. The 2001 report of Vice President Cheney's energy task force was only the most high profile in a series of pro-nuke developments. Nuke boosters are especially buoyed by more efficient plant designs, streamlined licensing procedures, and the prospect of federal subsidies.

In fact, new plants are on the way, however tentatively. Three groups of generating companies have entered a bureaucratic maze expected to lead to formal applications for plants by 2008. If everything breaks right, the first new reactors in decades will be online by 2014. If this seems ambitious, it's not; the industry hopes merely to hold on to nuclear's current 20 percent of the rapidly growing US electric power market.

That's not nearly enough. We should be shooting to match France, which gets 77 percent of its electricity from nukes. It's past time for a decisive leap out of the hydrocarbon era, time to send King Coal and, soon after, Big Oil shambling off to their well-deserved final resting places—maybe on a nostalgic old steam locomotive.

Material progress can be tracked in what gets pumped out of smokestacks. An hour of coal-generated 100-watt electric light creates 0.05 pounds of atmospheric carbon, a bucket of ice makes 0.3 pounds, an hour's car ride 5. The average American sends nearly half a ton of carbon spewing into the atmosphere every month. Europe and Japan are a little more economical, but even the most remote forest-burning peasants happily do their part.

And the worst—by far—is yet to come. An MIT study forecasts that worldwide energy demand could triple by 2050. China could build a Three Gorges Dam every year forever and still not meet its growing demand for electricity. Even the carbon reductions required by the Kyoto Protocol—which pointedly exempts developing countries like China—will be a drop in the atmospheric sewer.

What is a rapidly carbonizing world to do? The high-minded answer, of course, is renewables. But the notion that wind, water, solar, or biomass will save the day is at least as fanciful as the once-popular idea that nuclear energy would be too cheap to meter. Jesse Ausubel, director of the human environment program at New York's Rockefeller University, calls renewable energy sources "false gods"—attractive but powerless. They're capital-and-land-intensive, and solar is not yet remotely cost-competitive. Despite all the hype, tax breaks, and incentives, the proportion of US electricity production from renewables has actually fallen in the past 15 years, from 11.0 percent to 9.1 percent.

The decline would be even worse without hydropower, which accounts for 92 percent of the world's renewable electricity. While dams in the US are under attack from environmentalists trying to protect wild fish populations, the Chinese are building them on an ever grander scale. But even China's autocrats can't get past Nimby. Stung by criticism of the monumental Three Gorges project—which required the forcible relocation of 1 million people—officials have suspended an even bigger project on the Nu Jiang River in the country's remote southwest.

Solar power doesn't look much better. Its number-one problem is cost: While the price of photovoltaic cells has been slowly dropping, solar-generated electricity is still four times more expensive than nuclear (and more than five times the cost of coal). Maybe someday we'll all live in houses with photovoltaic roof tiles, but in the real world, a run-of-the-mill 1,000-megawatt photovoltaic plant will require about 60 square miles of panes alone. In other words, the largest industrial structure ever built.

Wind is more promising, which is one reason it's the lone renewable attracting serious interest from big-time equipment manufacturers like General Electric. But even though price and performance are expected to improve, wind, like solar, is inherently fickle, hard to capture, and widely dispersed. And wind turbines take up a lot of space; Ausubel points out that the wind equivalent of a typical utility plant would require 300 square miles of turbines plus costly transmission lines from the wind-scoured fields of, say, North Dakota. Alternatively, there's California's Altamont Pass, where 5,400 windmills slice and dice some 1,300 birds of prey annually.

What about biomass? Ethanol is clean, but growing the amount of cellulose required to shift US electricity production to biomass would require farming—no wilting organics, please—an area the size of 10 Iowas.

Among fossil fuels, natural gas holds some allure; it emits a third as much carbon as coal. That's an improvement but not enough if you're serious about rolling back carbon levels. Most of the work so far has been aimed at reducing acid rain by cutting sulphur dioxide and nitrogen oxide emissions, and more recently gasifying coal to make it burn cleaner.

By contrast, nuclear power is thriving around the world despite decades of obituaries. Belgium derives 58 percent of its electricity from nukes, Sweden 45 percent, South Korea 40, Switzerland 37 percent, Japan 31 percent, Spain 27 percent, and the UK 23 percent. Turkey plans to build three plants over the next several years. South Korea has eight more reactors coming, Japan 13, China at least 20. France, where nukes generate more than three-quarters of the country's electricity, is privatizing a third of its state-owned nuclear energy group, Areva, to deal with the rush of new business.

The last US nuke plant to be built was ordered in 1973, yet nuclear power is growing here as well. With clever engineering and smart management, nukes have steadily increased their share of generating capacity in the US. The 103 reactors operating in the US pump out electricity at more than 90 percent of capacity, up from 60 percent when Three Mile Island made headlines. That increase is the equivalent of adding 40 new reactors, without bothering anyone's backyard or spewing any more carbon into the air.

So atomic power is less expensive than it used to be—but could it possibly be cost-effective? Current operating costs are the lowest ever—1.82 cents per kilowatt-hour versus 2.13 cents for coal-fired plants and 3.69 cents for natural gas. The ultimate vindication of nuclear economics is playing out in the stock market: Over the past five years, the stocks of leading nuclear generating companies such as Exelon and Entergy have more than doubled. This remarkable success suggests that nuclear energy realistically could replace coal in the US without a cost increase and ultimately lead the way to a clean, green future. The trick is to start building nuke plants and keep building them at a furious pace. Anything less leaves carbon in the climatic driver's seat.

A decade ago, anyone thinking about constructing nuclear plants in the US would have been dismissed as out of touch with reality. But today, for the first time since the building of Three Mile Island, new nukes in the US seem possible. Thanks to improvements in reactor design and increasing encouragement from Washington, DC, the nuclear industry is posed for unlikely revival. "All the planets seem to be coming into alignment," says David Brown, VP for congressional affairs at Exelon.

The original US nuclear plants, built during the 1950s and '60s, were descended from propulsion units in 1950s-vintage nuclear submarines, now known as generation I. During the '80s and '90s, when new construction halted in the US, the major reactor makers—GE Power Systems, British-owned Westinghouse, France's Framatome (part of Areva), and Canada's AECL—went after customers in Europe. This new round of business led to system improvements that could eventually, after some prototyping, be deployed back in the US.

By all accounts, the latest reactors, generation III+, are a big improvement. They're fuel-efficient. They employ passive safety technologies, such as gravity-fed emergency cooling rather than pumps. Thanks to standardized construction, they may even be cost-competitive to build—$1,200 per kilowatt-hour of generating capacity versus more than $1,300 for the latest low-emission (which is not to say low-carbon) coal plants. But there's no way to know for sure until someone actually builds one. And even then, the first few will almost certainly cost more.

The US Department of Energy agreed in 2002 to pick up the tab of the first hurdle—getting from engineering design to working blueprints. Three groups of utility companies and reactor makers have stepped up for the program, optimistically dubbed Nuclear Power 2010. The government's bill to taxpayers for this stage of development could top $500 million, but at least we'll get working reactors rather than "promising technologies."

But newer, better designs don't free the industry from the intense public oversight that has been nuclear power's special burden from the start. Believe it or not, Three Mile Island wasn't the ultimate nightmare; that would be Shoreham, the Long Island power plant shuttered in 1994 after a nine-year legal battle, without ever having sold a single electron. Construction was already complete when opponents challenged the plant's application for an operating license. Wall Street won't invest billions in new plants ($5.5 billion in Shoreham's case) without a clear path through the maze of judges and regulators.

Shoreham didn't die completely in vain. The 1992 Energy Policy Act aims to forestall such debacles by authorizing the Nuclear Regulatory Commission to issue combined construction and operating licenses. It also allows the NRC to pre-certify specific reactor models and the energy companies to bank preapproved sites. Utility executives fret that no one has ever road-tested the new process, which still requires public hearings and shelves of supporting documents. An idle reactor site at Browns Ferry, Alabama, could be an early test case; the Tennessee Valley Authority is exploring options to refurbish it rather than start from scratch.

Meanwhile, Congress looks ready to provide a boost to the nuclear energy industry. Pete Domenici (R-New Mexico), chair of the Senate's energy committee and the patron saint of nuclear power in Washington, has vowed to revive last year's energy bill, which died in the Senate.   As pork goes, the provision is easy to defend. Nuclear power's extraordinary startup costs and safety risks make it a special case for government intervention. And the amount is precisely the same bounty Washington spends annually in tax credits for wind, biomass, and other zero-emission kilowattage.

Safer plants, more sensible regulation, and even a helping hand from Congress—all are on the way. What's still missing is a place to put radioactive waste. By law, US companies that generate nuclear power pay the Feds a tenth of a cent per kilowatt-hour to dispose of their spent fuel. The fund—currently $24 billion and counting—is supposed to finance a permanent waste repository, the ill-fated Yucca Mountain in Nevada. Two decades ago when the payments started, opening day was scheduled for January 31, 1998. But the Nevada facility remains embroiled in hearings, debates, and studies, and waste is piling up at 30-odd sites around the country. Nobody will build a nuke plant until Washington offers a better answer than "keep piling."

But throwing waste into a black hole at Yucca Mountain isn't such a great idea anyway. For one thing, in coming decades we might devise better disposal methods, such as corrosion-proof containers that can withstand millennia of heat and moisture. For another, used nuclear fuel can be recycled as a source for the production of more energy. Either way, it's clear that the whole waste disposal problem has been misconstrued. We don't need a million-year solution. A hundred years will do just fine— long enough to let the stuff cool down and allow us to decide what to do with it.

The name for this approach is interim storage: Find a few patches of isolated real estate—we're not talking about taking it over for eternity—and pour nice big concrete pads; add floodlights, motion detectors, and razor wire; truck in nuclear waste in bombproof 20-foot-high concrete casks. Voila: safe storage while you wait for either Yucca Mountain or plan B.

Two dozen reactor sites around the country already have their own interim facilities; a private company has applied with the NRC to open one on the Goshute Indian reservation in Skull Valley, Utah. Establishing a half-dozen federally managed sites is closer to the right idea. Domenici says he'll introduce legislation this year for a national interim storage system.

A handful of new US plants will be a fine start, but the real goal has to be dethroning King Coal and—until something better comes along—pushing nuclear power out front as the world's default energy source. Kicking carbon cold turkey won't be easy, but it can be done.

- Regulate carbon emissions. Nuclear plants have to account for every radioactive atom of waste. Meanwhile, coal-fired plants dump tons of deadly refuse into the atmosphere at zero cost. It's time for that free ride to end, but only the government can make it happen.
- Recycle nuclear fuel. Here's a fun fact: Spent nuclear fuel—the stuff intended for permanent disposal at Yucca Mountain—retains 95 percent of its energy content. Imagine what Toyota could do for fuel efficiency if 95 percent of the average car's gasoline passed through the engine and out the tailpipe. In France, Japan, and Britain, nuclear engineers do the sensible thing: recycle. Alone among the nuclear powers, the US doesn't, for reasons that have nothing to do with nuclear power.
- Rekindle innovation. Although nuclear technology has come a long way since Three Mile Island, the field is hardly a hotbed of innovation. Government-funded research—such as the DOE's Next Generation Nuclear Plant program—is aimed at designing advanced reactors, including high temperature, gas-cooled plants of the kind being built in China and South Africa and fast-breeder reactors that will use uranium 60 times more efficiently than today's reactors. Still, the nuclear industry suffers from its legacy of having been born under a mushroom cloud and raised by your local electric company. A tight leash on nuclear R&D may be good, even necessary. But there's nothing like a little competition to

spur creativity. That's reason enough to want to see US companies squarely back on the nuclear power field—research is great, but more and smarter buyers ultimately drive quality up and prices down.

- Replace gasoline with hydrogen. If a single change could truly ignite nuclear power, it's the grab bag of technologies and wishful schemes traveling under the rubric of the hydrogen economy. Leaving behind petroleum is as important to the planet's future as eliminating coal. The hitch is that it takes energy to extract hydrogen from substances like methane and water. Where will it come from?

Today, the most common energy source for producing hydrogen is natural gas, followed by oil. It's conceivable that renewables could do it in limited quantities. By the luck of physics, though, two things nuclear reactors do best—generate both electricity and very high temperatures—are exactly what it takes to produce hydrogen most efficiently. Last November, the DOE's Idaho National Engineering and Environmental Laboratory showed how a single next-gen nuke could produce the hydrogen equivalent of 400,000 gallons of gasoline every day. Nuclear energy's potential for freeing us not only from coal but also oil holds the promise of a bright green future for the US and the world at large.

The more seriously you take the idea of global warming, the more seriously you have to take nuclear power. Clean coal, solar-powered roof tiles, wind farms in North Dakota—they're all pie in the emissions-free sky. Sure, give them a shot. But zero-carbon reactors are here and now. We know we can build them. Their price tag is no mystery. They fit into the existing electric grid without a hitch. Flannel-shirted environmentalists who fight these realities run the risk of ending up with as much soot on their hands as the slickest coal-mining CEO.

America's voracious energy appetite doesn't have to be a bug—it can be a feature. Shanghai, Seoul, and San Paolo are more likely to look to Los Angeles or Houston as a model than to some solar-powered idyll. Energy technology is no different than any other; innovation can change all the rules. But if the best we can offer the developing world is bromides about energy independence, we'll deserve the carbon-choked nightmare of a planet we get.

Nuclear energy is the big bang still reverberating. It's the power to light a city in a lump the size of a soda can. Peter Huber and Mark Mills have written an iconoclastic new book on energy, The Bottomless Well. They see nuclear power as merely the latest in a series of technologies that will gradually eliminate our need to carve up huge swaths of the planet. "Energy isn't the problem. Energy is the solution," they write. "Energy begets more energy. The more of it we capture and put to use, the more readily we will capture still more."

The best way to avoid running out of fossil fuels is to switch to something better. The Stone Age famously did not end for lack of stones, and neither should we wait for the last chunk of anthracite to flicker out before we kiss hydrocarbons good-bye. Especially not when something cleaner, safer, more efficient, and more abundant is ready to roll. It's time to get real.

Calder Hill Nuclear Power Plant in the United Kingdom

ACTIVITY 4.4

RECONSIDER ATOMIC ENERGY

"How Clean, Green Atomic Energy Can Stop Global Warming" was originally published in *Wired* magazine in 2005. Since that date, the increasing price of fuel, particularly gasoline, makes an article on atomic energy even more timely. Do some informal research on the Internet to evaluate the kairotic appeal of atomic energy as an essay topic.

1. What is the status of the atomic energy debate today in the United States? In other parts of the world?
2. Does your research make this essay seem dated, or does it make the essay seem like a prediction?

INCLUDE IMAGES TO INCREASE KAIROTIC APPEAL

Kairos is about making use of the context of an argument—a particular moment in a specific time and place. If you were, for example, writing an essay about the causes of the 2008 "mortgage meltdown" and the resulting crisis in the United States, you could give your audience a more immediate sense of the time and place by including an illustration such as the one below from the *Economist*.

Source: *The Economist*, Sept. 20, 2008

This *Economist* photo vividly illustrates the reaction of one man on the floor of the New York Stock Exchange to one of the downturns in the stock market, and in one glance will make clear to your reader the seriousness of the financial crisis from the perspective of Wall Street. Although such an image is copyrighted, you can scan and import it into your essay without formal permission because it is a class assignment for educational purposes. You cannot, however, put it up on a web page or otherwise publish it without permission. You should credit the image by putting "Source: *The Economist*, Sept. 20, 2008" above your photo caption, and you should also include the image in your works cited page or list of references.

SOCIAL NETWORKING SITES UTILIZE TEXT AND IMAGES

Social networking sites such as Facebook and MySpace are used daily by millions of people to keep in touch with busy friends, business associates, and those who share common interests. Most social network sites allow members to create a profile for themselves and then have additional pages for contacts with friends or other topics. Some members choose to have closed or internal social networking which is members or "friends" only. Other sites allow open membership. Social scientists and rhetoricians have begun studying social networking sites because it is a new and different communication medium, but considering the millions using the sites on a daily basis, the sites seem destined to continue.

As the following article, "Does Facebook Replace Face Time or Enhance It?" suggests, social networking sites have created a new kairos, a different communication space with its own time, space, and protocols for communication. The author of the article, Lisa Selin Davis, finds that if she wants to connect with her friend Jenny, the only communication medium that works is Facebook. Jenny does not make phone calls, has no time for social visits, will not even email, but she constantly updates her Facebook page.

Facebook members interact but not face-to-face nor even usually in real time. You leave messages for friends, and friends respond when they have the time. One easy-to-access option lets you say what you are doing now, whether it is baking a cake or touring the old city in Jerusalem. Members post pictures of grandchildren, their pets, and recent travels. The kairos of Facebook is undemanding, stay-in-touch communication, with the option of sharing what you want of personal life. The loss may be "face time" but the gain is personal contact—of a sort. As Lisa Selin Davis explains, if you have friends who have become Facebook hermits, your choice is lose a friend or join Facebook.

**READING
4.3**

**"DOES FACEBOOK REPLACE FACE TIME
OR ENHANCE IT?"
BY LISA SELIN DAVIS**

Jenny has not returned my calls in roughly a year. She has, however, sent me a poinsettia, poked me and placed a gift beneath my Christmas tree. She's done all this virtually, courtesy of Facebook, the social-networking site on which users create profiles, gather "friends" and join common-interest groups, not to mention send digital gifts. Although Jenny has three children, ages 4 to 14, and rarely finds time for visits, phone calls or even e-mail, the full-time mom in upstate New York regularly updates her status on Facebook

("Jenny is fixing a birthday dinner," "Jenny took the kids sledding") and uploads photos (her son in the school play). After 24 years, our friendship is now relegated to the online world, filtered through Facebook. Call it Facebook Recluse Syndrome—and Jenny is far from the site's only social hermit.

Although Facebook started as an online hub for college students, its fastest-growing demographic is the over-25 crowd, which now accounts for more than half of the site's 140 million active members. Why is Facebook catching on among harried parents and professionals? "It makes me feel like I have a grip on my world," says Emily Neill, a 39-year-old single mother of two. Neill isn't a techie, per se—"I'll never have a phone that does anything but make calls," says the fashion consultant in Watertown, Mass.—but she stays logged on to Facebook all day at work and then spends an hour or two—or lately three—at night checking in with old acquaintances, swapping photos with close friends and instant-messaging those who fall somewhere in between. "It makes you feel like you're part of something even if you're neglecting people in the flesh," she says.

Retreating behind a digital veil started long before the Internet existed, with the advent of answering machines. "People would call a phone when they knew the other person wasn't available to pick up," says Charles Steinfield, a professor at Michigan State University who co-authored a peer-reviewed study called "The Benefits of Facebook 'Friends.'" "It enabled them to convey information without forcing them to interact."

Enter Facebook, which provides a constant flow of information via short updates from everyone a user knows: a distant cousin is glad he skipped the cheeseburger chowder; a colleague has a new book on sale; a close friend is engaged or newly single. Jenny and I, along with three of our childhood pals from Saratoga Springs, N.Y., learned that a dear old friend had ended her seven-year relationship through a Facebook status change. We expressed dismay, albeit through Facebook's IM feature, that we had to learn such potent information in this impersonal way.

Yet for many users, Facebook somehow remains distinctly personal. Although social-networking sites typically encourage connections among strangers—like on MySpace, where people converge through common interests, or online dating, where the whole point is to greet new faces—Facebook is geared toward helping people maintain existing connections. The site serves as a self-updating address book, keeping users connected no matter their geographical shifts. "There are people from my past life that I never would have tracked through 10 job changes and 20 e-mail changes," says Nicole Ellison, an assistant professor at Michigan State and lead author of the Facebook "Friends" study, which focused on undergraduate usage of the site. Facebook offers what she describes as a "seamless way of keeping in touch that doesn't involve all this work."

Perhaps this is the key. Jenny's online sociability and offline silence probably has less to do with digital retreating than time management. Facebook offers e-mail, IM and photo sharing in what Neill calls the "one-stop shopping" of online interaction. "It's not surprising to me that it's replacing other forms of communication," says Steinfield.

It's still surprising to me, however, this combination of Orwell and WALL-E that has humans watching one another through computer screens and socializing in quasi-isolation. Neill says Facebook has brought her closer to her already close friends, whom she has little time to see because of kids and work. "I know more about them now than I did when I was in regular contact with them," she says.

I believe her. But I can't help wondering: If for some reason Facebook suddenly ceased to exist, would people like Jenny revert to phone calls or visits, or would they lose touch altogether?

I probably won't find out. Instead, I gave in. Last week I sent Jenny a note—through Facebook, naturally—requesting a get-together. She accepted. When we met up, it seemed like we were closer than I had thought. I knew about Jenny's son's part in the school play, her sledding expedition and what she'd cooked for that big birthday dinner—information we would have shared if we still lived in the same neighborhood and talked regularly, the inane and intimate details that add up to life. The constant stream of data is a digital form of closeness. "A beautiful blossoming garden of information about your friends," as Neill puts it, adding, "I don't see how that can be a bad thing."

This Facebook page is centered around a book, *500 Years of Chicana Women's History*, by Elizabeth "Betita" Martinez. The Facebook group has more than 900 members who share an interest in the book and related issues. Facebook members often create pages for a personal interest and may choose to have the page open or closed to members.

ACTIVITY 4.5

DISCUSS THE KAIROS OF SOCIAL NETWORKING SITES

After reading "Does Facebook Replace Face Time or Enhance It?" discuss your experience with Facebook or another social networking site.

1. Describe what you do on Facebook or other social networking sites. How is it different from face-to-face communication with friends or associates?
2. Describe the kairos of the social networking site—the "context of a certain moment, a particular time and place."
3. What is the attraction of social networking sites that encourages millions of people to utilize them daily, even becoming social network "hermits"?
4. How are photos or other images used on social network sites to enhance communication? What purpose do they serve?

ASSIGNMENT: WRITE A RHETORICAL ANALYSIS

In this essay you will make use of rhetorical vocabulary to analyze a text or combined text and images. The student essay example in Chapter 7 analyzes a speech archived on the American Rhetoric website, http://www.american-rhetoric.com, which features many presidential and other prominent speeches. Alternatively, you can write a rhetorical analysis of a Facebook page, a newspaper or magazine article, or website.

In your analysis, apply several of the rhetorical concepts you have studied this semester:

*   Occasion for speaking (or writing)—What precipitated this text or speech?
*   Purpose—What was the speaker or writer trying to achieve?
*   Audience—Who was the speech/text directed to? Are there multiple audiences?
*   Rhetorical appeals: Ethos, pathos, logos.
*   Kairos—What is special about the rhetorical moment of the text/speech in terms of place and time?

Specifications for your essay:
- Suggested page length: 3-4 pages.
- Organize your essay with an introduction, body paragraphs, and closing.
- You may discuss the rhetorical concepts in any order you choose. You do not need to refer to all of them, but your paper should reflect an awareness of the rhetorical concepts.
- Be sure to include the name of the speaker, the title of the speech/text, the date it was presented or published, and the location of the presentation or publication.

Your analysis will be evaluated according to these criteria:
- How successfully are rhetorical concepts used to shed light on the topic?
- Have you provided a context for the speech/text? If you use additional sources, you may need to document them if they include opinions or information that are not common knowledge. Common knowledge is generally information that could be found in a number of sources, even if not everyone is familiar with the information.
- Does your essay have a clear thesis, whether or not it is stated or implied?
- Have you used several quotes from the speech/text and analyzed the quotes?
- How effective is the organization of the paper and coherence of the analysis?
- How well are major points explained and developed?
- Is the language clear, concise, and correct?
- Is the paper generally free from surface grammatical errors?

five

5

Establish *Ethos* through Research

Although the words "research paper" sound imposing to many students, research is really a natural part of your experience. You do research every day, often without being aware of the process, whether it is determining the calorie count of a serving of sugar-free ice cream or calculating the dollar amount you will spend on gasoline for a weekend trip. The information gathering you do for a research paper builds on the informal research skills you already have by adding additional places you look to for information and additional tools to use in that search. Today, researchers have available to them a staggering array of sources, including the traditional—library books and reference books—and newer online sources through library databases and websites.

Researching rhetorically, the title of this chapter, is to make use of your ethos or credibility as a writer by incorporating your expert knowledge because of everyday experiences and the subjects you have studied. It also involves maximizing and also "borrowing" the credibility of source materials you quote or paraphrase in your text. When you quote or paraphrase an expert, your paper gains authority that it would not otherwise have. For example, if you are the parent of a child with Attention Deficit Hyperactivity Disorder (ADHD), your experiences caring for that child and interacting with the health care and educational systems, as well as the reading you have done to seek out effective treatment, qualifies you to speak with authority about what it is like to raise such as child. If you are writing a paper about educational options for children with ADHD, you can cite some of your own experiences, but you will also want to quote or paraphrase opinions of authorities about the best ways to provide a quality educational environment. These opinions of experts can be found in books, periodicals, and possibly government documents, and including them will increase your power to convince an audience.

Academic research begins with what you know. If you've asked to write a paper on the environment, you probably know quite a few things about the environment already. Perhaps you belong to the local Sierra Club or other environmental organization or perhaps you are aware of a significant environmental issue in your community. In El Paso, for example, Asarco, a mining and smelting company, is attempting to reopen a copper smelting plant, closed since 1999, which is located on the Texas/Mexico border not far from the city's downtown. Recently, the Texas Commission on Environmental Quality granted Asarco a five-year air-quality permit, which would allow Asarco to resume copper smelting, though the reopening is opposed by community leaders. This topic would make an excellent research paper, particularly because there are arguments on both sides, in addition to the company's profit motive. Proponents say the reopening will return much-needed jobs to the city which were lost when the plant closed, while opponents claim that the plant will belch pollutants into the air, worsening the city's air quality.

Your own mind is often the best place to begin your research, as you probably have general knowledge of several contemporary topics, though they may not be at the forefront of your mind. The invention techniques discussed in Chapter 5 can help you access information recorded in your memory. Of course, information from general knowledge or personal experience is raw material that must be organized and refined in the writing process, so that its use enhances your *ethos* as a writer.

How do you go about finding the best reference sources to support your general knowledge? A key factor to keep in mind is the credibility of each of the sources you choose. Citing information from a source written in the last three years is generally more credible than from one published ten years ago because the information is obviously more current. Peer-reviewed journals and books published by reputable publishers are probably the most credible sources. Information from news magazines such as *Time, Newsweek,* or *U.S. News and World Report* has more credence than that from a popular magazine such as *Glamour* or *People* which are designed for entertainment rather than covering the news. Indeed, many instructors will forbid the use of Wikipedia as a source, not because all the information is inaccurate (because it is not) but because the reader has no way of evaluating whether information is correct or not since the entries were written by volunteers, and the content has not been vetted by a reputable publisher or other authoritative organization.

Don't be reluctant to ask for help. Your instructor may be willing to suggest resources on your topic, as will librarians. Instructors may refer you to specific books or authors. Others will demonstrate a Nexis journal search for you, in the process finding you valuable sources. Librarians also can be valuable allies in your search, as their job is to serve your needs as a library patron. If you ask for help, a librarian will often run a search for you in the online catalog or may even walk with you into the stacks to find appropriate source materials.

ACTIVITY
5.1
BEGIN WITH WHAT YOU KNOW

In your small group, make a list of controversial topics that you already have some knowledge about because of personal experience or course work. For example, one of you may be among the millions of Americans without health insurance or you may know someone who is. If so, you probably know about some of the failings of the American health care system. Alternatively, you may have lost a job during the 2009 recession or been unable to find a job when you needed one. If so, you probably have some thoughts about the efforts of the federal government to deal with the economic crisis. These personal connections with controversial issues give you a starting point for research on a topic. Share your group's list with the class.

PRIMARY AND SECONDARY RESEARCH

If you've bought a stereo lately, chances are you did some research when you decided which brand you would buy. To begin with, you already had some knowledge of stereo systems and brand names. Maybe you heard someplace that a particular receiver was good or that a certain speaker had a tendency to blow a woofer at high volumes. You listened to friends' stereos and you knew which brands are popular and which produce clear sound. You didn't have to look in a book for that information. It is just part of your everyday knowledge. You may not use it every day, but it's there when you need it.

Once you explored your knowledge of stereos by thinking about what you already knew, you probably visited a stereo showroom and listened to several stereos. Maybe you asked the salesperson about the model you were interested in, and asked friends about their stereos and how much they liked them. You might have consulted a buying guide that rates stereo equipment and gave you suggestions on the sound quality, reliability, and value of several different stereos. You might also have looked at a few reviews of equipment in magazines at a local bookstore. If you did any or all of these things, then you are already familiar with basic primary and secondary research.

Primary research involves personal interaction with your subject. Interviews from people on the scene of an event, questionnaires, and observation are all primary sources. Novels, poems, diaries, and fictional films are also primary sources because they stand alone and are not interpreting anything else. To return to the stereo analogy, when you listened to various stereos, you were doing primary research. When you asked people for opinions or read a buying guide, you were doing **secondary research**. Similarly, when you read a *Time* magazine article which analyzes climate change and quotes prominent experts in the field, you are consulting secondary research.

A little later in this chapter is a profile assignment that asks you to interview and observe someone who has some unusual life experience or interesting attribute. You may be able to gather all the information you need for this assignment by doing an interview and filling out the observation form in this chapter. If you have known the person previously, you may add references to that prior knowledge.

Other writing assignments ask you to combine your own experience or primary research with information gained from secondary research in books or periodicals. For example, you might be asked to write an essay about recycling. You can include your own experience with recycling or visit a recycling center in your community and report what you see. You can also support this primary research with secondary research in books or periodicals in which authorities offer facts and opinions about the effectiveness of recycling. In addition, you can interview an authority on recycling, perhaps a professor or chairperson of a community committee, an additional secondary source.

You may notice that many magazine articles or books refer to other books, statistical studies, or additional evidence but do not document sources in the text or give a bibliography. In this course, however, your instructor will probably ask you, when using outside references, to document them following the Modern Language Association (MLA) format. The purpose is to train you in academic writing, which differs in conventions from journalism or popular writing in that all sources are credited both in the text and in a works cited page. Documentation also benefits those who read your essays and might want to use the same sources for additional research of their own. It is, therefore, not a check against plagiarism but an important tool for other researchers.

INTERVIEWS

Depending on your topic, your community probably has some excellent sources sitting behind desks at the nearest college, city hall, or federal office building. If you are looking into the environment, you could contact the Environmental Protection Agency, an attorney who specializes in environmental law, a professional employee of the park system or the Bureau of Land Management, a college professor who works in the natural sciences, or a group in your area dedicated to beautification and restoration efforts. If you don't know anyone connected with these organizations, a look in the yellow pages or blue government pages of the phone book should give you the information you need.

When you contact the person you'd like to **interview**, identify yourself and your reason for wanting to speak with him or her. Most people are happy to assist college students in their research, and almost everyone is flattered by the attention. If your first choice refuses, ask him or her if they know anyone who might be knowledgeable about your topic and available for an interview. When you get a positive response, arrange an hour and a location convenient to both of you. If the interview is scheduled more than a week from the initial contact, you can write a letter confirming your appointment, or you can call the day before the scheduled interview to confirm the time and location.

Once you've scheduled the interview, make a list of questions you will ask your interview subject. There are two types of questions you can ask your subject: open and closed. **Open questions** such as the following leave room for extended discussion because they don't have a yes, no, or specific answer:

Could you tell me about the most positive experience you've had with [topic]?

When did you decide to study [topic]?

What's the most negative experience you've had with [topic]?

Questions like these allow for extended discussions. Even if it seems your subject has finished his or her response to the question, let a few moments of silence pass before you ask another question. Silence can be uncomfortable for some people, and he or she might feel compelled to expand on the response to your question in interesting ways.

Closed questions are useful for gathering specific information. Questions such as "When did you graduate?" and "How long have you been involved in [topic]?" are closed questions. Although closed questions are important to an interview, be sure they're balanced by questions that allow your subject room to talk and expand on his or her ideas.

Before the interview, confirm the exact location of your appointment. If you are unfamiliar with the planned meeting place, go by the day before to make sure you can find it. Take several pens or pencils with you to the interview in addition to a writing tablet with a stiff back. If possible, use a cassette recorder to tape the interview. Be sure to ask your subject if it is okay for you to tape. Most people will allow taping, if you assure them that the recording is only for your use in collecting information for your research paper. If you plan to record the interview, install fresh batteries and use a tape long enough to continue the interview for at least a half an hour past your planned length of the interview. If you are using a recorder, test its operation before you get to the interview location so you won't have any surprises when you're with your subject or discover later that the machine was not recording.

Although you've prepared a list of questions you'll want to follow, don't be afraid to ask a question that isn't on your list. If your subject mentions briefly an experience that seems relevant to your topic, you might want to ask him or her more about that experience, even though it isn't on your list of questions. Indeed, the best way to interview may be to read over your questions just before you meet your subject, then not refer to them during the interview. Before you leave, however, look over your list to see if you have missed any questions of importance. Remember to let lulls in the conversation work for you by drawing your interview subject into further explanations or illustrations of previous comments. If you interview a talkative person who strays from the topic, try to steer him or her back to the questions you've prepared, but if you can't, don't worry. You'll probably get useful information anyway. Be courteous and attentive. Even if you're recording the interview, take notes. It makes both the subject and the interviewer feel more comfortable and serves as a backup, should your recording not work.

Within fifteen minutes after leaving the interview, jot down some notes about your subject's appearance; the sights, sounds, and smells of the place where you conducted the interview; and any overall impressions of the meeting. Make sure you have the date and location of the interview in your notes because you will need it for documentation on your works cited page.

OBSERVATION

Close **observation** for descriptive detail can enhance almost any topic. If you are writing a paper on the effectiveness of recycling in your community, you might take a trip to your community's processing area for recycled glass. There you could gather information through senses about the glass process. You might also be able to conduct short, informal interviews with the employees about the process.

You may need to call to get permission to visit certain places. You'll need to identify yourself and your topic. Usually you can get permission to visit and observe. However, if you cannot get permission to visit an area, you can ask your contact if there is a similar area nearby. Again, look at your research questions before you visit to decide which questions might be answered by your observations. For example, if you have read about recycling centers in other communities, during your visit to the local center, you could observe the similarities and differences in their procedures. Good writers always have more detail than they actually use, so they have choices about what to include.

The key to successful observation is tuning the senses. Can you remember what your room smelled like when you woke up this morning, the first thing you saw when you opened your eyes, the way your sheets or blanket felt against your skin, the sounds in the room after you turned off your alarm, or the taste of orange juice or coffee you had with breakfast? Our minds are trained to ignore seemingly unimportant information, so if you can't remember any sensory details from your morning, you're not alone. When conducting an observation, however, those sensory responses are an important part of your research. Sitting in the place you're observing, freewrite for at least five minutes on each of the senses: touch, taste, smell, sight, and sound. You might even freewrite on each of the senses from several different vantage points, depending on the size of the place or event you're observing. Take notes on the responses given to you from anyone you speak with.

Within fifteen minutes after you've left the place you've been observing, take a few minutes to read over your notes and write a few overall impressions or add details you've missed in your description. Look again at your research questions and decide which ones have been answered by your visit.

**ACTIVITY
5.2**   **OBSERVATION EXERCISE**

In this exercise, describe your classroom. Alternatively, go to another setting such as a museum, restaurant, or library and describe that space and the people in it.

- How large is the space, approximately? Describe the shape of the room, color and texture of walls, ceiling, and floor.
- How is the space furnished? Describe the color, shape, and style of the furnishings.
- What about representing the other senses? Is the room silent or noisy? Does it have a characteristic smell? Describe.
- How many people are in the room? What are they doing? Describe their ages, general style of dress, and possessions such as computers, backpacks, or purses.
- Pick two or three people that stand out in some way from the other occupants and write a sentence or two about each, describing what it is about each person that caught your attention.

**ACTIVITY
5.3**   **WRITE A PROFILE OF A PERSON OR PLACE**

Write a profile of a person or place that is unusual in some way. Your **profile** should include description, quotes, and whatever background explanations are needed to provide a context, so that the story flows logically from one element to another. The length should be approximately 750 to 1000 words. Answering the following questions will help you elicit information you need to write your profile.

1. **History**—What is the history of the person or place or thing? Does the history affect the present?
2. **Qualities**—What qualities make this person worth writing about? Can you give examples that *show* the qualities?
3. **Values and Standards**—What does the subject believe in most strongly? How does this shape his/her actions? Can you give specific examples?

4. **Impact**—How does the subject affect those around him or her? This may include both positives and negatives. Give examples.
5. **Description**—Write a physical description of the person, including any unusual aspects that make the person stand out in a crowd. Describe the setting where you interviewed the person or where the person works or lives.

SECONDARY RESEARCH SOURCES PROFESSORS EXPECT

You have been assigned a research paper or project. What does your professor expect of you? First of all, that you understand the assignment: What specifically does your professor want you to research? Do you have instructions about what kinds of sources your professor wants? Are restrictions put on what Internet or database sources you can use? Possibly, your instructor has specified that you need to use books, journals, major magazines and newspapers, and certain web-based information. This means that you are to use reputable sources to obtain a balanced, impartial viewpoint about your topic. So, how do you find these sources?

Books: In these days of easy-to-find resources on the Internet, students may wonder why to bother with books at all. However, scholarly books treat academic topics with in-depth discussion and careful documentation of evidence. College libraries collect scholarly books that are carefully researched and reviewed by authorities in the book's field. Look for recently published books rather than older books, even if they are on your topic. Academic books or well-researched popular books often have bibliographies or lists of additional references at the end of the book. These lists are useful for two reasons: first, if such lists of books are present, it is a good clue this is a well-researched book, and, second, it gives you a ready list of other possible resources you can consult for your research project.

Scholarly journals: Just having the word "journal" in the title does not mean it is a journal. *Ladies Home Journal,* or the *Wall Street Journal,* for example, are not journals. Your instructor means peer-reviewed journals in which the authors have documented their sources. Peer-reviewed means that articles have been reviewed by experts in the field for reliability and relevance before being published. Your library should have print indexes to journals in which you can look up your topic. You may also be able to find journal articles—sometimes in full text—through the online databases offered by your college library.

Major magazines and newspapers: These publications report the news based on actual observation of events and interviews with experts and also present informed editorial opinions. Examples are magazines such as *Time, Newsweek,* and *U.S. News and World Report;* newspapers such as the *New York Times,* the *Boston Globe,* the *Wall Street Journal,* and the *Washington Post.* You can locate full-text articles directly from the online versions of major print magazines and newspapers. Often, these publications charge a fee for articles not published recently. However, you can often find the same articles free through one of your library databases.

Special Interest Publications: These are periodicals that focus on a specific topic but are written for a wider audience than are scholarly journals. Authors of articles base their articles on interviews with experts, recent scholarly books and journals, and other reputable sources. Examples include *Psychology Today* and *Scientific American.*

Government Documents: Government documents present a wealth of information for many contemporary events and issues. Your library may be a federal depository, which means that users can locate many federal documents onsite. If so, you can look up government sources in the online library catalog. Government documents are also available though online databases.

Encyclopedias: Encyclopedias can be useful to browse when you are looking for topics. They are also helpful for providing background information such as dates when events occurred. However, most instructors prefer that you do not use encyclopedias as sources you cite in your paper. This is particularly true for Wikipedia, the online encyclopedia that is assembled by volunteers who have specialized knowledge on topics and, thus, has no systematic vetting of the contents. However, Wikipedia entries often include bibliographies which can be useful in pointing you to books, articles, or other websites which can be used as references.

Internet: The problem with web-based information is that anyone with some knowledge of computers can put up a website on the Internet. Thus, information from websites must be carefully evaluated as to author, publishing organization, etc. One way to deal with this problem is to find web information through the librarian-generated indexes and search engines which screen websites for credibility (See list later in this chapter).

As you use the categories above to find sources for your paper or project, realize that your topic influences your choice of reference materials. If you are writing about a literary topic such as Shakespeare's *Othello*, you will find a number of relevant books and journal articles. If your topic is more contemporary, such as the current status of the country's housing market, you may be able to find some books or journal articles for background information, but you will need to use recent magazine and newspaper articles to find the latest information.

As you examine your sources, remember that gathering the information should help you discover what you think about your topic, not just what others think. This will enable you to create a paper based on your ideas and opinions, with source materials supporting your position.

Employ Computerized Library Catalogs

Public Access Catalogs (PACs) or computerized catalogs have replaced card catalogs. A library computerized catalog provides bibliographical information about the library's collection, including thousands of books, photos, videos, journals, and other items. Generally, catalogs can be accessed by keyword, subject, author, title, and call number. You may also find books which are available in digital form through the catalog. In addition, on the library home page, you will find links to other information and services such as database searches, interlibrary loan, and course reserves.

Types of Computerized Searches

- **Keyword**—*Unless you know the author or title of a book, keyword is the best type of search because it finds the search word or words anywhere in the bibliographical citation.*
  Example: water quality

- **Title**—*Type the exact order of words in the title.*
  Example: History of the United Kingdom
- **Author**—*Type the author's name, putting the last name first. You don't need to include a comma.*
  Example: Miller Henry J.
- **Subject**—*Type the exact Library of Congress subject heading.*
  Example: Spanish language—Grammar, Historical
- **Call Number**—*Type the exact call number.*
  Example: B851 .P49 2004

If you have a general topic, you probably want to use the keyword search, for subject search actually refers to the Library of Congress subject-search designations, and, unless you use precisely the search terms specified by that classification system, you may not get the results you want. Using keywords, however, will lead you to hits on your topic. Then, once you have found one book that is in your topic area, you can examine the screen for Library of Congress subject headings and click on those to browse for more books.

An invaluable resource of any library is the Interlibrary Loan Department. Here you can request books your library does not own, as well as journal articles from periodicals not in the library's collection or obtainable through the library's databases.   Books and articles are obtained for you by the staff on a minimal or no fee basis. This is extremely helpful because you can request books you find in bibliographies. However, it generally takes seven to ten days to obtain books through interlibrary loan, so you need to plan well in advance. To request an item, you simply go to the Interlibrary Loan Department in your library or fill out a form on the library's website.

ACTIVITY 5.4

LOCATE BOOKS ON YOUR TOPIC

Using the online card catalog at the library, locate three books about your topic. Write down the titles, authors, publishers and dates of publication. Also write the catalog numbers. Now, go to the stacks and find the books. While you are there, find two other books nearby on the same topic. Check the table of contents and index to see if they contain information you can use.

Utilize Electronic Library Resources

College and university libraries increasingly rely on databases to provide digital versions of articles published in journals, magazines, newspapers, government documents, as well as other publications and materials. Generally, the databases are available to students and faculty through the Internet via the library home page, though a library card and a password may be required for off-campus access.

Library databases make use of online forms similar to those of a library computerized catalog. Searches are by subject, title, author, and name of publication. Advanced search features are available. Some databases provide full text of articles published in newspapers, journals, and magazines. Others give publication information only, such as title, author, publication, date of publication, and an abstract of the article. Popular databases include Lexis-Nexis, Academic Search Complete, Periodical Archive Online (ProQuest), Project Muse, and JSTOR.

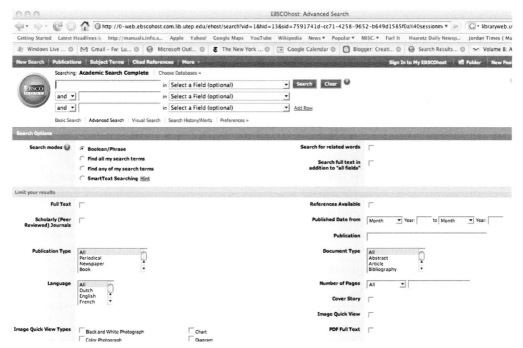

Academic Search Complete is one of EBSCO's popular online databases that can be accessed by students through their library's website. The database indexes full-text articles on a wide variety of topics.

ACTIVITY 5.5   LOCATE NEWSPAPER AND MAGAZINE ARTICLES

Go to your library's online databases and locate one that relates to your topic. Once you find one, access it and type in your topic. Try using various key words. Jot down titles, authors and publication information concerning any articles that look interesting. If full-text versions are available, email them to yourself. If not, find out if your library has hard copy or microfilm of the articles.

FIND INTERNET INFORMATION

The World Wide Web is an incredible resource for research. Through it, you can find full texts of pending legislation, searchable online editions of Shakespeare's plays, environmental impact statements, stock quotes, and much, much more. Finding credible research sources is not always easy. Anyone with an Internet connection and a little knowledge can put up a webpage and claim to be an expert on a chosen topic. Therefore, information from the Internet must be scrutinized with even more diligence than do print sources. For example, if you enter the word "environment" in one of the keyword search engines, you may receive thousands of "hits," or sites that relate to that topic from all over the world. How do you sift through all of that feedback in order to find information relevant to your topic? It is a problem that has not been completely solved on the Internet.

However, the search engine Google now provides Google Books, http://books.google.com, that offers full-text of millions of books, though usually not full-text of the entire book unless the book is no longer copyrighted. Also, Google Scholar, http://scholar.google.com, provides access to scholarly papers, though if your library has computerized databases, it will likely have a more extensive collection available to you. Also, the Directory of Online Open Access Journals, http://www.doaj.org, enables you to search online journals that offer free access.

One of the best ways for students to find Internet resources is through several indexing projects sponsored by major libraries. In the case of each directory/search tool, librarians have personally reviewed and selected websites that are of value to academic researchers, including both students and faculty. These indexing websites may be organized by subject area, in addition to having keyword search engines. Thus, you might quickly locate the most authoritative websites without having to wade through masses of sites looking for the reliable ones.

Librarians' Index to the Internet, http://lii.org
Internet Public Library, http://www.ipl.org
Infomine, http://infomine.ucr.edu

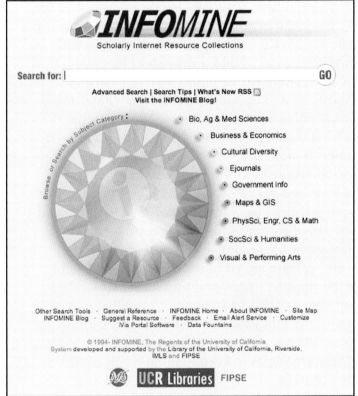

Infomine, http://infomine.urc.edu, is one of the librarian-generated sites on the Internet which collects links to scholarly resources in a variety of fields.

Government Documents can also be found easily through the Internet and are indexed at a variety of sites, including these:

FirstGov, http://www.firstgov.gov
Thomas Legislative Information, http://thomas.loc.gov
Federal Citizen Information Center, http://www.pueblo.gsa.gov/
FedWorld.Gov, http://www.fedworld.gov/

EVALUATE SOURCES

Many people tend to believe what they see in print. They may think that if information is in a book or a news magazine, it must be true. If you read critically, however, you know that all sources must be evaluated. With the Internet, perhaps even more than with print texts, it is important to evaluate your sources. Here are some guidelines to consider when evaluating sources.

- **Who is the author?** This question is equally important, whether the source in question is a book, a magazine, or a website. If you have the dust jacket of the book, the back flap will quickly provide you with essential information to screen the author. In the short biographical sketch, usually included along with a photo, you can learn the author's academic credentials and university affiliation, what previous books the author has published, and other qualifications that the publisher thinks qualifies the author to write this particular book. If there is no dust jacket (as is often true with library books), you can try to find information about the author through an Internet search engine or a reference text such as *Contemporary Authors*. A magazine or journal will often provide brief biographical information at the end of the article or on a separate authors' page. If the text is on a website, determining the authorship is more complex, as authors often are not named. In that case, you are forced to rely on the credibility of the entity publishing the website. Many websites have a link called something like "About Us" or "Mission Statement," and that page will give you some idea about the motivations of the entity sponsoring the site. Are they selling something? Is it part of an organization that has a political agenda? These are things to keep in mind when considering the bias of the site's content.
- **For what audience is the text written?** Determining this may require some detective work. In the case of a book, the preface or introduction may give you some clues. With magazines and journals, consider the demographics of the readership. With a website, a little clicking around in the site should tell you from the kind of texts, graphics, and advertising (if any), what readers the site is designed for.
- **What sources does the author rely upon?** If you are working with an academic text, the sources should be clearly cited in the text

by author and page number, footnotes, or endnotes. If it is a more popular book or article, sources are acknowledged less formally; however, a credible author will still make an effort to credit sources. For example, an article might say, "According to the March issue of the *New England Journal of Medicine*...."

- **Does the text have an obvious bias?** Ask yourself if the argument is logical and if sources are mentioned for any statistics or other evidence. Are any opposing viewpoints discussed fairly? Does the author engage in name calling, a clear sign of bias? Are there obvious holes or contradictions in the argument? For most purposes, you are looking for texts which do not appear to have been written with a biased agenda. However, in some cases, the opposite is true. If you are looking for a political candidate's position on a certain issue, then reading the candidate's book or going to the candidate's website will provide you with a biased viewpoint but one which you can analyze for the purposes of your paper. When dealing with information from sources with an obvious agenda, though, you must be careful not to represent the material as unbiased in your text.

- **What do others think of the text?** For a book, you can look for a review in *Book Review Digest* or *Book Review Index*, two publications you can find in the reference section of the library. Also, the *New York Times* and other newspapers review prominent popular books. Most magazines and newspapers print letters to the editor which may offer comment on controversial articles. The Scout Report, which can be found at the *Scout Project*, http://scout.wisc.edu, reviews selected websites. If you locate a review of your text, you can cite the review in your research paper to provide additional evidence of the text's degree of credibility.

**ACTIVITY
5.6**   **LOCATE AND EVALUATE A SOURCE**

Locate one source (book, magazine or newspaper article, or website page) which you think would be a credible source for a research paper. For that source, answer the questions above in the Evaluate Sources section.

ASSIGNMENT:
PREPARE AN ANNOTATED BIBLIOGRAPHY

An **annotated bibliography** is a list of bibliographical citations with a few sentences or a paragraph for each entry that offers explanatory information or critical commentary about the source. Many instructors request annotated bibliographies as a step in writing a research paper because it is an indication of the scope and direction of your research.

1. Select ten quality sources about your topic. These should be, as your instructor directs, a mix of books, scholarly journal and magazine articles, government documents, and selected texts from websites.
2. Skim the text of each source and read portions more closely that seem relevant to your topic.
3. Write a bibliographical citation for each source in MLA style (See the appendix for MLA style samples).
4. Write a few sentences for each source in which you do the following:
   a.) Summarize the content and purpose of the source.
   b.) Explain how you might use the source in your research paper.

SAMPLE ANNOTATED BIBLIOGRAPHY ENTRY:

Lewin, Tamar. "U.S. Universities Rush to Set Up Outposts Abroad."
    New York Times. New York Times Co., 8 Feb. 2008. Web. 15 Feb. 2008.

In the Middle East, American universities are competing to establish branch campuses where students can earn American university degrees. Already, in Qatar, programs are being offered by Cornell, Georgetown, Carnegie Mellon, Virginia Commonwealth, and Texas A&M Universities. This article demonstrates the appeal of the American university educational system to students from other countries.

6

USE THE TOOLS OF A SKILLED RHETOR

At the end of one semester, one student reflected on what she'd learned during the semester. She said:

> I used to sit down to write, and whatever ended up on the page was what I typed and handed in. I had no concept of the invention process and the difference it could make in the content of the essay. This became clearer when I completed our final essay. The invention work was instrumental in helping me remember vivid details, people, even my feelings, all of which were important components of the paper.

This student is on the path toward becoming a skilled rhetor. Already, she has learned how spending time on activities *before* writing can help her writing. She is learning methods that can help improve her writing, similar to how students of rhetoric in ancient Greece and Rome studied the art of composition as a way of learning to be effective orators, an essential skill for a citizen in those cultures.

THE FIVE PARTS OF RHETORIC

Greek and Roman rhetoricians divided rhetoric into five parts or "faculties" that correspond to the order of activities involved in creating a speech: **invention, arrangement, style, memory,** and **delivery**. These five parts, or **"faculties," of rhetoric** are described in many handbooks of rhetorical instruction, including the *Rhetorica ad Herennium* which was composed by an unknown author between 86 and 82 C.E.:

> The speaker ... should possess the faculties of Invention, Arrangement, Style, Memory, and Delivery. Invention is the devising of matter, true or plausible, that would make the case convincing. Arrangement is the ordering and distribution of the matter, making clear the place to which each thing is to be assigned. Style is the adaptation of suitable words and sentences to the matter devised. Memory is the firm retention in the mind of the matter, words, and arrangement. Delivery is the graceful regulation of voice, countenance, and gesture.

Today, classes in composition or writing studies still emphasize the necessity of **invention**, now interpreted as pre-writing activities that enable writers to develop the logic and words needed for effective arguments. **Arrangement** currently involves organizing an argument into a logical format that leads the reader easily from the thesis to the conclusion. **Style** has to do with the author's voice, tone, and structure of sentences and paragraphs. **Memory** is used somewhat differently today, as students are no longer required to memorize compositions for oral presentation. Instead, memory is utilized in ways such as remembering how and where to retrieve information from the Internet, books, and other reference materials. Finally, **delivery**, which once involved gestures and tone of voice in an oral presentation, today has to do with document design, so that the final product is presented in a professional manner according to Modern Language Association (MLA) or American Psychological Association (APA) style. Delivery also involves grammatical accuracy because surface errors detract from the effective impact of a document.

Table 6.1

THE FIVE PARTS (OR "FACULTIES") OF RHETORIC		
ENGLISH	GREEK	LATIN
invention	*heuresis*	*inventio*
arrangement	*taxis*	*dispositio*
style	*lexis*	*elocutio*
memory	*mneme*	*memoria*
delivery	*hypocrisis*	*actin*

THE WRITING PROCESS OVERVIEW

When you are planning to write, what do you do? Do you talk to a friend about the topic you are writing about, or do you go to the library to look up what experts have said about your topic? Do you write in your head as you drive to school, or do you sit at your kitchen table with your favorite pen and create an extensive outline before you begin typing your paper into the computer? Do you only write a sentence down when you know it is perfect, or do you allow words to flow on to the page unedited, checking for spelling and grammar errors later? Do you ask people to read and respond to your writing, or are you hesitant even to show it to your instructor? Maybe you put off writing until the evening before your paper is due; then you sit down to write at midnight, hoping you will finish before breakfast.

Every writer, even the student writer, has developed habits of writing. These habits may help a writer complete thoughtful and well-written essays, or they may keep a writer from doing his or her best work. No matter what habits you have developed, examining the habits of successful writers can help you get better ideas and write more thorough and thoughtful essays. It is likely your instructor will ask you to follow a set of steps in order to write your essays for this class. The steps the instructor asks you to follow are not just random requirements. Instead, they have come from careful analysis of the activities of successful student and professional writers.

INVENTING

Writing is not only about putting the pen to paper. As did rhetors in ancient Greece and Rome, you have to think deeply and critically about the subject before you begin a composition. The "invention" step of the writer's process is designed to help you find a worthwhile topic and develop your ideas about that topic before you start to write a draft. It includes writing, discussion, and research, as well as informal writing to help you explore your thoughts and feelings about a subject. Whatever method you choose, keep a record of your thoughts and the discoveries that come up as you spend this time in close examination of your subject.

DRAFTING

It may seem odd that writing a draft should come in the middle of the writer's process. However, research has shown that students and professionals alike write more effective essays when they don't reach for the pen too quickly. If you have spent enough time in the invention stage, the actual drafting stage may go more quickly. You write the first draft, then in succeeding drafts you add details, observations, illustrations, examples, expert testimony, and other support that will help your essay entertain, illuminate or convince your audience.

REVISING

Today, we talk more about the revision stage of writing than did ancient rhetoricians. If your habits have included writing your class essays at the last minute, you may have missed this step entirely, yet many writers claim this is the longest and most rewarding step in the writing process. To revise, you must, in a sense, learn to let go of your writing. Some students think their first drafts should stay exactly the way they are written because they are true to their feelings and experience. Many writers find, however, that first drafts assume too much about the reader's knowledge and reactions. Sometimes readers, reading a first draft essay, are left scratching their heads and wondering what it is the writer is trying to convey. Writers who revise try to read their writing as readers would note gaps in logic, absence of clear examples, need for reordering information, etc. Then they can revise content with the reader in mind.

EDITING AND POLISHING

Once writers have clarified their messages and the methods by which they get their points across, one more step must be taken. Particularly because their compositions are written, rather than oral presentations, they must go over their work again to check for correct spelling, grammar, and punctuation, as well as the use of Standard Written English. Some students finish with an essay, print it, and turn it in without ever examining the final copy. This is a critical mistake, because misspelled words, and typographical and formatting errors can make an otherwise well-written essay lose credibility.

USING *TOPOI* TO DEVELOP A TOPIC INTO AN ESSAY

Students in ancient Greece, like modern students, generally began the composition process with a subject or topic and then explored the topic from a variety of perspectives or viewpoints, something like our contemporary prewriting process. For example, they would define terms and the meanings associated with those terms, and then consider the moral connotations of those meanings. Aristotle and other teachers of rhetoric did this by employing "**topoi**" which might be translated literally as "places" or more generally as "topics." A *topoi* is a strategy or heuristic made up of questions about a topic which allows a rhetor to construe an argument. *Topoi* applicable to any topic are sometimes called common topics or commonplaces. Following is an outline of Aristotle's common topics which can be applied to develop research paper topics into essays. It is based upon a schema developed by Edward P.J. Corbett and Robert J. Connors for *Classical Rhetoric for the Modern Student*.

In each case, you would answer the question and then elaborate on your answer. In the process of answering the questions, you may develop an approach to discussing the topic.

QUESTIONS OF DEFINITION

Genus or classification—*What larger class does your subject belong to? If, for example, you are writing about stem cell research, the larger class might be medical ethics.*

Species or division—*What makes your topic unique in terms of its class? For stem cell research, you might discuss embryonic stem cells as different from adult stem cells.*

QUESTIONS OF COMPARISON

Similarity—*What characteristics does your topic share with others? How is the stem cell research controversy similar to other medical controversies such as the use of animals to test new drugs and medical procedures?*

Difference—*What makes your topic unique? How is it different from others? How does research with stem cells differ from other medical research controversies?*

Degree—*How significant are those similarities and/or differences?*

Cause and Effect—*What makes your topic happen? What are the consequences of your topic and how significant are they? Embryonic stem cells were chosen for research because they have not yet differentiated into cell types such as heart cells or skin cells and, thus, offer more opportunities for modification into cells that can be used for medical treatment. A consequence of the use of embryonic stem cells, however, is that it involves the destruction of human embryos.*

QUESTIONS OF RELATIONSHIPS

Antecedent and Consequence—*What came before your topic? What will happen because of it? In other words, you might ask the question of your subject: "If your topic occurs, then what?" For example, if the embryos come from fertility clinics and were to be destroyed anyway, is there a problem with using them for research? Some argue that a consequence of using embryonic stem cells is that it opens the door to cloning human cells.*

Contraries—*What is the argument that proves the opposite of your argument? For example, instead of arguing that embryonic stem cells should or should not be used for research, you might argue that diseases should not be treated by alteration of genetic material. Thus, no stem cells should be used for research.*

Contradictions—*What other interpretations could there be of your topic? If your topic is not what you think it is, what else might it be? For example, early on, stem cell researchers feared that the public would protest "the technological power" of stem cells, questioning what would happen if someone put human stem cells into the brain of a rat. Would you have a human mind in a rat's brain?*

QUESTIONS OF CIRCUMSTANCE

Possible and Impossible—*How feasible and/or workable is your topic? What factors make your topic either possible or impossible? For example, you can question whether it is moral to leave unexplored medical research that could lead to cures for diabetes and other major illnesses.*

Past Fact and Future Fact—*What precedents are there for your topic? Has it happened or been tried before? Based on past experience, what can you predict for the future of your topic? Based on other medical research, how feasible is it that using embryonic stem cells could lead to cures for diseases?*

QUESTIONS OF TESTIMONY

Authority—*What sources of information do you have to support your topic? What makes your sources authoritative? For example, have you based your argument upon recognized medical authorities? Are there those in the medical community who might disagree? Indeed, are medical leaders the proper authorities for your argument?*

Testimonial—*Who has personally experienced your topic? How might their experience enhance or detract from the credibility of your position on your topic? Do you have examples of the testimony of couples who have donated embryonic cells to this research? Do you have testimony of individuals who have diabetes and other diseases that might be cured by such research?*

Statistics—*What documented research can you find that gives insight about your topic? How widespread or significant is your topic? Do you have statistics that result from studies using embryonic vs. adult stem cells? Do you have statistics about the diseases that may be receptive to treatment with stem cells?*

ACTIVITY 6.1

USE *TOPOI* TO EXPLORE YOUR TOPIC

After you have chosen your general topic, answer each of the questions developed from Aristotle's *topoi*, beginning with "Questions of Definition." For each question that seems relevant to your topic, elaborate your answer in three or four sentences. Use this information generated about your topic to narrow or broaden your topic as you develop your thesis.

OTHER INVENTION STRATEGIES

Great myths have grown up around writers who can supposedly sit down, put pen to paper, and write a masterpiece. If these myths had developed about any other type of artist—a musician or a painter—we would scoff about them and ask about the years of study and practice those artists had spent before they created their masterpieces. Since all of us can write to some degree, perhaps it seems more feasible that great authors simply appear magically amongst us. Alas, it is not so; like all talented artists, good writers must learn their craft through consistent and continuous practice. Similar to how the ancient Greeks used *topoi* to generate raw material for their compositions, many writers today use the following invention strategies as prewriting activities:

FREEWRITING
One practice method developed in the 1970s and often attributed to Peter Elbow, author of *Writing Without Teachers*, is called *freewriting*. And

the method is just what it sounds like—writing that is free of any content restrictions. You simply write what is on your mind. Freeform, but there is some structure—you must set a time limit before you begin, and once you begin, you must not stop. The time period is usually ten to twenty minutes, and you must keep your pen or pencil moving on the page—no hesitations, no corrections, no rereading. Don't worry about spelling, or punctuation, or grammar—just download onto the paper whatever comes to mind. It will seem awkward at best; some have said it is downright painful. But after a few weeks practice, you will realize it is effective, and a wonderful individual method of getting at your thoughts on a subject.

INVISIBLE FREEWRITING

If you just cannot stop paying attention to your spelling and grammar, or if you find yourself always stopping to read what you have written, you can **freewrite invisibly**. To do this, you will need carbon paper and a pen that is retracted or out of ink. You sandwich the carbon paper, carbon side down, between two sheets of paper and write on the top sheet with your empty pen. You cannot see what you are writing, but you will have it recorded on the bottom sheet of paper. You can easily modify this to work on the computer by taping a blank sheet of paper over the monitor while you type.

FOCUSED FREEWRITING

When freewriting, you are writing without sticking to any particular topic. You are exploring many ideas and your sentences may roam from your day at work, the letter you just got from your sister, or a story you read in the paper about a man who tracks the nighttime migrations of songbirds. With **focused freewriting,** you are trying to concentrate on one particular subject. You can write that subject at the top of the page to remind you of your topic as you write. The rules are the same, but when you are focusing, you are more aware of exploring one question or idea in depth.

One drawback of focused freewriting is that students sometimes confuse it with a different step in the writing process, drafting. Remember that freewriting is "invention" work, intended only to help you explore ideas on paper. Drafting takes place only after you have explored, analyzed, and organized those ideas. Freewriting helps you think and write critically about a topic while drafting occurs once you have done the critical thinking necessary to come up with a unified, cohesive, and organized plan for an essay.

LISTING/BRAINSTORMING

This method of mapping is the least visual and the most straightforward. Unlike freewriting, where you write continuously, with **listing** you write down words and/or phrases that provide a shorthand for the ideas you might use in your essay, much as you would a grocery or "to-do" list. *Brainstorming* is a bit looser. Lists usually follow line after line on the page; brainstorming consists of words and phrases placed anywhere on the page you want to write them down.

CLUSTERING

When you think of a cluster, you think of several like things grouped together, often with something holding them together. *Peanut clusters*, a type of candy, are peanuts joined together with milk chocolate. *Star clusters* are groupings of stars, like the Pleiades or the Big Dipper connected by their relative positions to each other in space. You can create **clusters** of like ideas by grouping your ideas around a central topic on a blank sheet of paper.

ORGANIZING OR ARRANGING

The "invention" process is intended to get our ideas out of our heads and onto a piece of paper, but rarely do these ideas arrive in the most logical or effective order. Take some time (an hour or so for a short essay) to analyze your inventions. Place all the ideas in a logical order, and join similar ideas. Next, look for your most significant point, the most important thing you want to say about your subject. This may become your tentative thesis. Then identify which of the other items on your list will help you communicate your point and delete items that are irrelevant to your thesis.

ACTIVITY
6.2   FOCUSED FREEWRITING

1. Write your topic at the top of a blank sheet of paper.
2. Write a list of at least ten aspects or characteristics of your topic.
3. Choose two or three items from your list and do a focused freewriting on each item for five to eight minutes.
4. Add more items to your list if you have discovered new ideas during your freewriting.

ESTABLISH AN OCCASION FOR WRITING

Why do writers write? To express ideas. To persuade an audience. To respond to an event in their lives. To learn new ideas. To discover themselves. You may be able to add other motivations to the list. Combine one of these personalized motivations with a topic and an audience, and you have an occasion for writing. You may think that you do not need to be concerned about an occasion for writing because the text and perhaps your instructor provide you with assignments. Do not be misled, however. Assignments as phrased in this textbook or as given by your instructor are not in themselves occasions for writing.

ACTIVITY 6.3

STATEMENT OF OCCASION FOR WRITING

To write your statement of your occasion for writing, create the following three headings on a piece of paper. After each heading write two or three sentences about how your topic relates to each of them.

Purpose: Why are you writing about this topic?
Writer: How does this topic affect you?
Audience: Who is your audience and what effect do you want to have on your audience?

At this point in the writing process, your statement of occasion for writng may be rather rough or tentative. However, verbalizing these topics will help you as you move to the next stage of the process.

ORGANIZE YOUR ESSAY

Classical rhetoricians based their teaching of arrangement, or organization of a composition, upon the practices they noticed among the most outstanding orators of their day. The basic arrangement of material then is much the same as familiar organization today. An orator would begin by attracting the audience's attention in what they called the *exordium* which we would call the opening or introduction. Next, they would provide background information in a *narratio* or narration, followed by an *explication* in which they would define terms and enumerate the issues. During the *partition* they would express the thesis or main issue to be discussed, and in the *confirmation* they would provide evidence to support the thesis. Opposition arguments would be addressed in the *refutatio*, and the composition would be wrapped up with a *peroratio* or conclusion. The order of these different elements was not rigid in ancient times, nor is it today, and sometimes one or more sections were eliminated if they were not needed, but then, as now, an effective text included most of these elements. For example, if your audience is very familiar with a particular subject, you would not need to define terms, as you would with an audience who was unfamiliar with the material.

As you begin to draft your research paper, you might want to keep the elements of an effective composition in mind, perhaps checking as you complete your first draft to be sure either that all are present or that there is a reason for eliminating one or more parts. Like the ancient Greeks, you will begin with an opening and end with a conclusion. However, in between the bookends of your essay, you will likely want to rearrange the elements somewhat, as we have done in the discussion that follows in the chapter.

ELEMENTS OF EFFECTIVE ORGANIZATION FROM ANCIENT RHETORIC

Opening (Exordium): *Attracts the audience's attention to the issue.*

Background or narration (Narratio): *Details the history or facts of the issue.*

Definition or explication (Explicatio): *Defines terms and outlines issues.*

Thesis (Partitio): *States the particular issue that is to be argued.*

Proof (Confirmatio): *Develops the thesis and provides support evidence.*

Refutation or opposition (Refutatio): *Addresses the arguments opposing the thesis.*

Conclusion (Peroratio): *Reiterates the thesis and may urge the audience to action.*

WRITE A THESIS STATEMENT

A **thesis** may be a sentence or a series of sentences, or in a few cases may be implied rather than stated explicitly; but a thesis is at the heart of a piece of writing. If a reader cannot identify your thesis, the meaning of your text is not clear. How do you develop a thesis? First, you determine your occasion for writing—who is your audience, what is your purpose, and what special circumstances are there, if any. Then you write a working thesis that makes an assertion or claim about your topic, something that will be affected by your audience and purpose. For example, if you are writing a research paper about the advantages and disadvantages of biodiesel fuel, your claim may be stated differently if your audience is an English class than if it is a chemistry class. In the latter, you might need to use technical language that would be unfamiliar to your English professor.

Working theses are statements that develop and change as essays are written; they are basic frameworks which provide a connection for the ideas you have decided to convey to your reader. Later, after you have completed a draft of your text, examine your working thesis. If needed, rewrite your thesis so that it clearly states the main idea of your essay in a clear and engaging fashion.

EXAMPLES OF A THESIS STATEMENT

The United States should implement a guest worker program as a way of reforming the illegal immigration problem.

Nuclear power should be considered as part of a program to reduce the United States' dependence on foreign oil.

COMPOSE AN INTRODUCTION

Experienced writers have different methods of creating a good introduction. One who tends to discover his paper as he goes along swears the best way to write an introduction is write the entire paper, then move the conclusion to the beginning of the essay and rewrite it as the introduction. Another writer lets the paper sit around for a few days before she writes her introduction. A third always writes two or three different introductions and tries them out on friends before deciding which to use. However you choose to write the introduction, make sure it is interesting enough to make your reader want to read on.

The introduction to your essay is an invitation to your reader. If you invite readers to come along with you on a boring journey, they won't want to follow. In magazine and newspaper writing, the introduction is sometimes called a hook because it hooks the reader into reading the text. If a magazine writer does not capture the reader's attention right away, the reader is not likely to continue. After all, there are other and possibly more interesting articles in the magazine. Why should readers suffer through a boring introduction? Depending on the topic and pattern of your essay, you might employ one of the following techniques to hook your readers and make them keep reading:

- An intriguing or provocative quotation
- A narrative or anecdote
- A question or series of questions
- A vivid sensory description
- A strongly stated opinion

Your introductory paragraph makes a commitment to your readers. This is where you identify the topic, state your thesis (implicitly or explicitly), and give your readers clues about the journey that will follow in the succeeding paragraphs. Be careful not to mislead the reader. Do not ask questions you will not answer in your paper (unless they are rhetorical questions). Do not switch topics from your introduction to your paper.

Although the introduction is the first paragraph or so of the paper, it may not be the first paragraph the writer composes. If you have problems beginning your essay because you cannot immediately think of a good introduction, begin with the first point in your essay and come back to the introduction later.

COMBINE YOUR IDEAS WITH SUPPORT FROM SOURCE MATERIALS

A research paper, by definition, makes use of source materials to make an argument. It is important to remember, however, that it is *your* paper, *not* what some professors may call a "research dump," meaning that it is constructed by stringing together research information with a few transitions. Rather, you, as the author of the paper, carry the argument in your own words and use quotes and paraphrases from source materials to support your argument. How do you do that? Here are some suggestions:

- After you think you have completed enough research to construct a working thesis and begin writing your paper, collect all your materials in front of you (photocopies of articles, printouts of electronic sources, and books) and spend a few hours reading through the materials and making notes. Then, put all the notes and materials to the side and freewrite for a few minutes about what you can remember from your research that is important. Take this freewriting and make a rough outline of main points you want to cover in your essay. Then you can go back to your notes and source materials to flesh out your outline.

- Use quotes for three reasons: 1.) You want to "borrow" the ethos or credibility of the source. For example, if you are writing about stem cell research, you may want to quote from an authority such as Dr. James A. Thomson, whose ground-breaking research led to the first use of stem cells for research. Alternatively, if you are quoting from the *New England Journal of Medicine* or another prestigious publication, it may be worth crediting a quote to that source. 2.) The material is so beautifully or succinctly written that it would lose its effectiveness if you reworded the material in your own words. 3.) You want to create a point of emphasis by quoting rather than paraphrasing. Otherwise, you probably want to paraphrase material from your sources, as quotes should be used sparingly. Often, writers quote source material in a first draft and then rewrite some of the quotes into paraphrases during the revision process.
- Introduce quotes. You should never have a sentence or sentences in quote marks just sitting in the middle of a paragraph, as it would puzzle a reader. If you quote, you should always introduce the quote by saying something like this: According to Dr. James A. Thomson, "Stem cell research......"
- Avoid plagiarism by clearly indicating material that is quoted or paraphrased. See the appendix for more information about citing source material.

Support Your Thesis

After you have attracted the interest of your audience, established your thesis and given any background information and definitions, you will next begin to give reasons for your position, which further develops your argument. These reasons are, in turn, supported by statistics, analogies, anecdotes, quotes from authorities which you have discovered in your research or know from personal knowledge. Ideally, arrange your reasons so that the strongest ones come either at the beginning or the end of this portion of the paper and the weaker ones fall in the middle which are not points of emphasis.

Answer Opposing Arguments

If you are aware of a contradicting statistic or other possible objection to your argument, it may be tempting to ignore that complication, hoping your audience will not notice. However, that is exactly the worst thing you can do. It is much better to anticipate your audience's possible questions or objections and address them in your discussion. Doing so prevents you from losing credibility by appearing to deceive your audience or from the perception that you are not aware of all the facts. Also, acknowledging possible refutations of your position actually strengthens your position by making you seem knowledgeable and fair-minded.

Vary Your Strategies or Patterns of Development

When composing your essay, you have many different strategies or **patterns of development** available to you. You may write entire essays whose strategy is argumentation or comparison and contrast, but more often, will combine many of these different modes while writing a single essay.

- Analysis entails a close examination of an issue, a book, a film, or other object, separating it into elements and examining each of the elements separately through other writing modes such as classification or comparison and contrast.
- Argumentation involves taking a strong stand on an issue supported by logical reasons and evidence intended to change a reader's mind on an issue or open a reader's eyes to a problem.
- Cause and effect is an explanation of the cause and subsequent effects or consequences of a specific action.
- Classification entails dividing and grouping things into logical categories.
- Comparison and contrast examines the similarities and differences between two or more things.
- Definition employs an explanation of the specific meaning of a word, phrase, or idea.
- Description uses vivid sensory details to present a picture or an image to the reader.
- Exemplification makes use of specific examples to explain, define, or analyze something.
- Narration uses a story or vignette to illustrate a specific point or examine an issue.

WRITE A CONCLUSION

After they have read the last paragraph of your essay, your readers should feel satisfied that you have covered everything you needed to and you have shared an insight. You may have heard the basic rules: A conclusion cannot address any new issues, and it should summarize the main points of the essay. Although these are valid and reliable rules, a summary is not always the best way to end an essay. The prohibition against new ideas in the final paragraph also might limit certain effective closures like a call to action or a question for the reader to ponder.

One effective technique for writing a conclusion is to refer back to your introduction. If you began with a narrative anecdote, a sensory description, or a question, you can tie a mention of it to your ending point. Or, if you are composing an argumentative essay, you might choose to summarize by using an expert quote to restate your thesis, giving the reader a final firm sense of ethos or credibility. You might also end with a single-sentence summary followed by a suggestion or a call to action for the reader. Another effective way to end an argument can be a paragraph that suggests further research.

A conclusion doesn't have to be long. As a matter of fact, it does not even need to be a separate paragraph, especially if your essay is short. If your closing comments are related to the final paragraph of the essay, one or two sentences can easily be added to the final body paragraph of the essay.

ASSIGNMENT:
WRITE A RESEARCH-BASED ARGUMENT PAPER

The Purpose of the Assignment

Writing a research paper gives you the opportunity to practice key academic writing skills, including locating and utilizing research materials, prewriting, drafting, and revision. It also requires you to take a position on a topic, create an argument, and support it with quotes and paraphrases from authoritative sources.

Purpose as a Writer

Your purpose as a writer is to convince readers to consider your argument carefully, and, if possible, to persuade them to your point of view. To do this, include appropriate background material and definitions, as well as a consideration of opposing arguments.

Topic

Your topic should address a current issue about which you can take a position and support in the paper length your instructor specifies. Choose your topic carefully, as it should be one that engages your interest and enthusiasm.

Audience

Unless your instructor specifies otherwise, you can assume that your audience has general awareness of your issue but is unfamiliar with scholarly sources on the topic.

Sources

To do your research, you will need to utilize **recent** and **credible** sources that include a mix of recent books, scholarly articles, public speeches, and news articles. You may also use interviews, observation, and personal experience, if it is relevant to your topic. Sources will be cited in the text and in a works cited page or references page according to MLA or APA style. Information gathered from your sources is to support the argument you have created. It is **not** an assignment in which you take information from sources and simply reorganize them into a paper. The expectation for this course is that you will use your sources to create an argument that is distinctly your own.

Thesis

Your essay should have a clear thesis that takes a position on an issue that can be supported within the word limitations of the assignment.

Rough Draft

As directed by your instructor, bring two copies of your rough draft essay to class for peer editing. The draft should have your sources credited in the text and should have a works cited page or references page.

Final Draft

Submit your final draft in MLA or APA format in a folder with your rough draft and copies of all of your source materials with the location of quotes or paraphrased material highlighted. If you are using material from a book or books, copy enough of the text before and after your quotes or paraphrases, so that your instructor has a context.

seven

ROLE OF REVISION

In ancient times, the focus of the rhetor was upon presentation of oral arguments in the form of speeches, and students trained to perform in pressured situations before a law court or assembly. Though a speaker might spend time in preparation, most speeches were one-time opportunities. If the words were not well-chosen and well-spoken the first time, there was no second chance to influence an audience.

With modern written documents, a composition does not have to be perfect when the words first appear on the page. A document is not truly finished until it is transmitted to an audience, and, even then, important documents are often circulated in draft stages to colleagues for comments before the process is complete, and it is presented to an audience.

Many writers claim that revising is the most rewarding step in writing, the time when they have words on a page to work with and can manipulate them to create a composition which communicates effectively. Yet, many students feel that their first drafts should stay exactly the way they've written them because these writings are truest to their feelings and experience.

They are sure they have made their point clearly, but the reader may be left scratching his or her head and wondering what it was the writer meant to say. To communicate effectively, a writer must learn to interact with his reader to ensure he has communicated his message clearly.

BEGIN REVISION BY REREADING

The first step of revising is rereading. This step can be simple, if you are reading something written by someone else, but when it is your own writing it becomes infinitely more difficult. After all, you know what you meant to say—you know the research behind the writing and why you chose certain words or phrases. You even know how every sentence is supposed to read—even though you left out a word or two or three—and your mind can trick you into seeing the missing words right where they belong. Unfortunately, the reader does not have your understanding, and communication can break down. You need to learn to read your own work critically, as if it were written by a stranger. One of the first aids in this process is to read your work aloud. You can often hear stumbling blocks, quicker than you can see them.

You can also learn to read your own work more objectively by reading and commenting on other writers' work. Look at the structure of essays, at the way the writers use transitions and topic sentences, and at the sentence structure and choice of words. As you learn to see how good writers put ideas and words together, you will begin to think about the readings in a more thorough manner—thinking of alternative, perhaps even better, ways to express the message of each essay. You will also learn to read your own work with a more critical eye.

QUALITIES OF EFFECTIVE WRITING

Reading the work of some professional writers, you may have developed the idea that the best writing is writing that is difficult to understand, writing that sends the reader to the dictionary with every sentence, or writing that uses many technical or specialized terms. Often, we think something difficult to read must be well written. Although it is sometimes difficult to read about topics that are new to us because we're learning new vocabulary and struggling with complex ideas, it simply is not true that the best writing is hard to read. Indeed, the most effective writing, the kind of writing you want to produce in your classes, is simple, concise, and direct.

KEEP IT SIMPLE

Simple means "unadorned" or "not ornate." *Writing simply* means saying something in common, concrete language without too much complication in the sentence structure. Writing simply doesn't mean you have to use only short or easy words. It doesn't mean that all your sentences will be simple sentences. It doesn't mean that you can't use figures of speech or intricate details. Simple writing means that you try to get your point across in a direct and interesting way. You aren't trying to hide your ideas. Instead, you are trying to amplify those ideas and begin an intelligible conversation with your reader.

Rely on Everyday Words

When writing about computers or other technical subjects, it's tempting to use *jargon* or specialized words you might use when talking to others with the same knowledge, interest, and background. When writing for a limited audience whose members are familiar with technical terms, a bit of jargon might be acceptable. However, most of the writing you will do in college and later in the workplace will address a larger audience. You will want to avoid the use of highly technical terms, acronyms, and abbreviations.

If it seems that the writers in this text use many big words or technical terms, stop for a minute to consider the original audience for each of the essays. Consider how your vocabulary grows each year as you read, discuss, and consider new ideas. The everyday words of a tenth grade student will probably be fewer in number than the everyday words of a junior in college. Similarly, the everyday words of a college freshman will be different from the everyday words of a computer professional with three years of work experience. Use words that are comfortable and familiar to you and your readers when you write, and you will write clear, effective essays.

Use Precise Words

We sometimes assume that our reader will know what we mean when we use adjectives like "beautiful," "quiet," or "slow." However, the reader has only his or her own ideas of those adjectives. You can make your writing more interesting and effective by adding the concrete details that will give the reader an image using at least two of the senses.

You can use details from all of the senses to make your writing more concrete, more precise. What are some of the sensual qualities of the experience or thing? Can you compare it to another thing that your readers may be familiar with to help them understand it better? Can you compare it to something totally unlike it? Can you compare it to a different sense to surprise the readers and help them understand the image you are trying to create?

A good way to practice your ability to write original concrete images is to expand on a cliche. A *cliche* is an overused saying or expression. Often, cliches begin as similes that help make images more concrete. They become cliched or overused because they lose their originality or they don't contain enough detail to give us the entire picture. Choose a cliche and write a sentence that expands the cliche and uses the senses to create a clear picture of the thing described. You might try some of the following cliches:

> She is as pretty as a picture.
> It smelled heavenly.
> It was as soft as a baby's bottom.
> His heart is as hard as stone.
> It tastes as sour as a pickle.
> We stared at the roaring campfire.
> We listened to the babbling brook.

Precise details allow us to experience the world of the writer. We leave our own views and perceptions and learn how someone else sees the world. What "quiet" is like for one writer. What "beautiful" means to another. Fill in the gaps between your words and ideas with vivid images and your writing becomes more interesting and more effective.

BE CONCISE

Rid your writing of excess words and leave only that which makes your meaning clear and concrete. Becoming aware of several common problems can help you make your writing more concise. When you begin a sentence with either "it is" or "there is," you transfer all the meaning of the sentence to the end of the sentence. This is known as a *delayed construction*. You have delayed the meaning. The reader must read on to find out what "it" or "there" refer to. They don't get anything important from the beginning of the sentence.

Examine the following sentences:
> It is important to change the oil in older gasoline engines.
> There is an apple on the table.
> There isn't anything we need to fear except our own fear.

We can rewrite these sentences, making them more concise, by deleting the "there is" or the "it is" and restructuring the sentence.

Changing the oil in older gasoline engines is important.

An apple is on the table.

We have nothing to fear but fear itself.

Notice that the second group of sentences is shorter and the important information is no longer buried in the middle. Revising this type of sentence can make your writing more concise and get information to the reader more effectively.

If you're afraid you use "it is" and "there is" (or "it's" and "there's") too often, you can use most word processing programs to seek these constructions out. Use the "search" or "find and replace" tool that's found in the Edit portion of your pull down menu. Type "it is" and ask your computer to find every place you use this construction in your document. When you find a sentence that begins with "it is," revise the sentence to make it more concise. Do the same with "there is," "it's," and "there's." After you become more aware of these errors by correcting them, you'll find that you notice the errors before or as you make them. You will begin to write more concisely, and you'll have fewer delayed constructions to revise.

You can also make your writing more concise by avoiding common wordy expressions. Sometimes when we're nervous about writing or insecure about our knowledge of a topic, we try to hide that insecurity behind a wall of meaningless words, such as does the following sentence:

At this point in time, you may not have the ability to create a web page due to the fact that you've avoided using computers for anything other than playing Solitaire.

This sentence is full of deadwood phrases that add no meaning to the sentence. If we take out the unneeded words, we have this sentence:

You may not be able to create a web page because you've only used your computer to play Solitaire.

Your computer may have a grammar checker that will identify some commonly used wordy expressions. If your computer doesn't have a grammar checker, or if your instructor has asked you not to use the grammar checker in your computer, you can still learn to revise the wordiness out of your paragraphs. Use the computer to separate a paragraph of your writing into sentences. As you scroll through the paragraph, hit the "hard return" or "enter" key on your keyboard twice every time you find a period. Once you have separated the sentences, look at each sentence. What is the important idea in the sentence? What words are used to convey that idea? What words don't add any meaning to the sentence? Delete words that don't convey meaning, and revise the sentence to make it more concise.

USE ACTION VERBS

Action verbs are words that convey the action of a sentence. They carry much of our language's nuance and meaning. Many inexperienced writers use only "to be" verbs: *am, is, are, was, were, be, been,* and *being.* If you use too many of these verbs, you risk losing much of the power of language. If I say someone is coming through the door, I've created a picture of a body and a doorway. If I say someone marches or slinks through the door, I've added not only the information about movement but also about the qualities of that movement. I've given my subject the attitude of a soldier or a cat. For example, consider this sentence written by Howard Rheingold:

> Thirty thousand years ago, outside a deceptively small hole in a limestone formation in the area now known as southern France, several adolescents shivered in the dark, awaiting initiation into the cult of toolmakers.

By using the verb "shivered," especially when accompanied by the words "in the dark," Rheingold paints a word picture much more vivid than he would have conveyed with the use of a "to be" verb. Using interesting verbs can enliven your writing.

If you want to focus upon using more action verbs, skim through your essay and circle all the "to be" verbs. Read the sentences with circled "to be" verbs more closely, and choose several to rewrite using active verbs in place of the "to be" verbs. You won't be able to do this for every sentence, but replace them where you can and your writing will become more lively, more concise, and more effective.

FILL IN THE GAPS

When we write, we sometimes forget that we are writing to an audience other than ourselves. We expect that our readers are people just like us, with our experiences, memories, and tastes. Because they're so much like us, we sometimes expect readers to be able to read more than what we've written on the page. We expect them to read our minds. We may leave large gaps in our essays, hoping the reader will fill in with exactly the information we would have included.

If I'm writing an essay about my childhood in the South and I say it was always so hot in the summer that I hated to go outside, I might think my reader knows what I mean by hot. However, there are many different ways to be "hot." In east Texas where I grew up, the hot was a sticky hot. Eighty degrees made me long for a big glass of sweetened iced tea with lots of ice. The heat made my clothes cling. Sweating didn't help because the sweat didn't dry. I spent the day feeling as if I'd never dried after my morning shower. In New Mexico, I never really felt hot unless the temperature got above 110 degrees. At that point, the heat would rush at me, making it difficult to breathe. I would open the door to leave the house, and it felt as if I had opened the oven door to check on a cake. If I say I was hot in the summer without describing how heat felt to me, my reader may not get the message I'm trying to convey. Don't expect your reader to know what you mean by "hot" or by any other general description. Instead, take a minute to add details that will fill in the gaps for the reader.

SPEAK DIRECTLY

To *speak directly* is to say, up front, who is doing what. Sometimes we don't tell the reader who is completing the action or we tell them too late. Let's look at the following sentences:

The steak was stolen from the grill.

The decisive battle was fought between the Confederate and the Union armies in Vicksburg, Mississippi.

The red truck has been driven into the side of the green car.

Although we might be able to guess who the actors are in each of the sentences, the first and last sentences don't tell us directly. Even if the reader can guess that it was a dog who stole the steak from the grill or my neighbor who drove the red truck into the side of the green car, the reader has to stop and figure out who is doing what before he or she can read on. This slows the reader down and diminishes the effectiveness of your writing.

Language professionals call this ***passive voice***. The action comes before the actor. Note that sometimes, as in the first and last sentences above, the writer doesn't mention the actor at all. These are tests for passive verbs:

- Look for verbs coupled with another action word that ends in "-ed" or "-en" such as "was stolen" or "was forgotten."

- Find the action and the actor in the sentence to make sure that they are in the most effective order. The most effective sentence order is actor first, then action. If the sentence does not specify the actor but leaves it implied, chances are that it is a passive sentence. For example, read this sentence: "The red truck was driven into the green car." It does not say who was the driver, and, thus is a passive sentence.

Rewriting some of your sentences with passive voice will make your writing stronger and more interesting.

President Barack Obama has won high marks for his verbal eloquence, as illustrated by this cartoon published in the *International Herald Tribune.* His 2004 Keynote Speech at the Democratic National Convention and his best-selling book *The Audacity of Hope* helped propel him to national prominence.

REMEMBER TO PROOFREAD

It is understandably difficult to find the errors in an essay you have been working on for days. A few tricks used by professional writers might help you see errors in your essay more clearly.

1. With pencil in hand, read the essay aloud, slowly, preferably to an audience. When you are reading aloud, it is more difficult to add or change words, so you tend to catch errors you would not see reading silently to yourself. Plus the reactions of your audience may point out areas where future readers may become confused or lose interest.

2. Another trick is to read the essay backwards, sentence by sentence. This forces you to look at sentence structure and not at the overall content of the essay. If you are working on a computer, another way to accomplish this is to create a final edit file in which you hit the hard return twice at the end of every question or statement. You might even go so far as to number the sentences so they look more like grammar exercises. Then look at each sentence individually.

GAIN FEEDBACK BY PEER EDITING

Your instructor may schedule class periods for peer workshops. These workshops are opportunities for you to get responses from your readers. Often, you will be divided into groups of three or four students and you will be given a list of questions to answer about your peers' essays. Your peers will get copies of your essay, and they will give you comments as well. The first peer workshop can be a difficult experience. It is never easy to take criticism, constructive or not. Taking criticism in a small group is even more difficult. There are several things you can do to make your peer groups more productive.

WHEN YOUR ESSAY IS BEING REVIEWED

1. Write down everything the reviewers say. You think you will remember it later, but often you will forget just that piece of advice you need. More importantly, writing while the reviewers speak is an effective way to keep the channels of communication open. It is hard to come up with a defense for your paper if you are busy writing.

2. Save your comments until all the reviewers are done. If you have specific questions, write them in the margins of your notes. If they ask you questions, make a note to answer them when everyone is done. If you allow yourself to speak, you will be tempted to start defending your essay. Once you start defending your essay, two things happen. First, you stop listening to the comments. Second, you offend your

reviewers, making it less likely that they will give you honest criticism in the future.

3. The first comment you should make to your reviewers is "Thank You." The second comment can be anything but a defense. Your readers are only telling you how they interpret your essay. They are giving you their opinions; you do not have to make the changes they suggest.

4. Save all the comments you get on your essay. Set them aside for a day or so. Then make the changes that you think will make your essay better.

WHEN YOU ARE THE REVIEWER

1. Read an essay through, at least one time, just to browse the content of the essay. Appreciate the essay for what it does well. Try to ignore any problems for now. You will get back to them the second time you read and begin your comments in the margins. Every essay will have at least one thing good about it.

2. Always begin your comments with a sincere discussion of what you like about the essay.

3. Be specific in your comments. Your peers will probably understand you better if you say, "The topic sentence in paragraph four really sets the reader up for what the essay accomplishes in paragraph four. But I can't really find a topic sentence for paragraph six, and the topic sentences in paragraphs two and three could be improved." Note how this statement gives a positive response and then identifies specific places where the author can improve the essay. This works much better than a generalized statement like, "Topic sentences need work."

4. Be descriptive in your comments. It is often helpful for students to hear how you are reading their essays. "Paragraph five seems to be telling me . . . " or "I got the feeling the essay's overall message is..." are good ways to start descriptive sentences.

5. Realize that you are analyzing a paper and not a person. Directing your comments toward the essay, "Paragraph nine doesn't really have anything new to add, does the paper need it?" sounds better to the listener than "You repeat yourself in paragraph nine. Do you really need it?"

INDEPENDENT REVIEWING

If your instructor does not require peer editing, you can ask someone to review your essay. Choose someone you trust to give you an honest opinion. It might not be effective to ask a parent, spouse, or girlfriend/boyfriend to give you a critique if you know they are going to like anything you write, just because you wrote it. It might be better to ask another student who has recently had an English class, or is enrolled in yours currently. In exchange, you might offer to look over their work. Remember, you learn to read your own essays better by reading other peoples' essays more critically.

SAMPLE QUESTIONS FOR PEER REVIEW

When you have revised your paper several times, have someone answer these questions for overall content, paragraph development, and word choice and sentence structure.

OVERALL CONTENT
1. What is the thesis or main point of the essay? Where does the writer state this main point? If the main point is implied rather than stated, express it in a sentence. Does the main point give a subject and an opinion about the subject? How might the writer improve his/her thesis?
2. What is the purpose of this essay? What are the characteristics of the audience the writer seems to be addressing? (formal, fun-loving, serious, cynical, laid-back, etc.)

PARAGRAPH DEVELOPMENT
1. Do each of the paragraphs in the essay work to support the main point of the essay? Which paragraphs seem to wander from that main point? What other information needs to be added to develop the main point?
2. List two places in the essay where the writer uses vivid sensory details. How effective are those details? Are they used to support the thesis of the essay? Identify two places in the essay where the writer needs more details that are effective. What kind of details might he or she include?

---

3. What grade would you give the introduction? How does it draw the reader into the essay? What specific things can the writer do to make the introduction more inviting?
4. Which paragraph do you like the best? Why? Which paragraph in the essay do you like the least? Why? What can the writer do to improve his/her paragraphs?
5. What grade would you give the conclusion? How does it provide closure for the essay? What specific things can the writer do to make the conclusion more effective?

WORD CHOICE AND SENTENCE STRUCTURE

1. Are adequate transitions used between the paragraphs? Find an effective paragraph transition and identify it. Why does it work? Find two places between paragraphs that need more or better transitions. What can the writer do to improve these transitions?
2. Is a variety of sentences used? Where might the writer vary the sentence structure for better effect? What two sentences in the essay did you find most effective? Why?
3. Are there any words that seem misused or out of place? What positive or negative trigger words are used? Do they enhance the message of the essay or detract from it?

ASSIGNMENT:
PEER EDITING OF SAMPLE STUDENT ESSAY

As your instructor directs, either individually or in groups, peer edit one of the following sample student papers, answering all the questions in the **SAMPLE QUESTIONS FOR PEER REVIEW** section. Then discuss your peer editing in your small groups, comparing your answers to others in your group.

SAMPLE STUDENT ESSAY FOR PEER EDITING, PROFILE ASSIGNMENT

LONGING FOR BETTER DAYS

As she sits in her cramped room in Amman, Jordan, watching the recent news, Aysha Mustafa, 92, is saddened by the world she lives in today. As she places her wrinkled hands on her lap and begins to recall a time where things were pleasant, tears begin to flow down her cheeks. Those times are long gone she says. Aysha moved from Palestine to Jordan after the sudden death of her husband in 1995. Moving here was tough she says, "It was hard to leave my country." Aysha's story goes back 60 years ago, where she lived in her homeland Palestine. She recalls her childhood as being peaceful and joyous. She smiles as she describes memories of her and her brother riding in the back of her father's wagon. "Life was good," she says. Although her family had very little to live on, she was still happy.

Like many Palestinians, Aysha still dreams to one day return back and live in her homeland Palestine, where she longs to rekindle sweet memories there. "Jordan is fine she says but I rather live on the land that is mine." As we sit in the living room watching the crisis in Gaza in January 2009, Aysha begins to wipe the tears from her sad yet hopeful eyes, and reiterates with a sigh in her voice, "May God be with them." The appalling images of young children being killed by Israeli rockets leave 92 year old Aysha in distress. How many more men, women and children will die before both sides reach an agreement she questions? As her grandson flips through the channels, he crosses upon the Al-Jazeera news that announces that the number killed in Gaza has reached the disturbing number of 781. She suddenly lowers her head and gazes into space. . "It kills me to see my people getting killed like this," she stutters trying to hold back tears. The Israeli and Palestinian conflict has been going on for more than 60 years now. Many innocent civilians of both sides have been killed due to this grotesque war.

Despite all of this, it is people like Aysha that still carry hope that one day they will return back to their homeland and live in peace and harmony. Aysha's wish like many others is for all Palestinians to live a life of security and freedom, freedom to make their own choices and decisions on their own land. Aysha struggles to explain how as a child she used to run around in the fields freely, fearing no one or anything. "The feeling of freedom is indescribable," she says. "I was free to walk and go as I pleased, with no blockades to hold me back."

Today however, boys and girls in Palestine do not share the same luxury that Aysha experienced before the occupation. It is heart breaking watching this old yet strong willed woman recalling her childhood memories. Suddenly, Aysha begins to hold her chest and breathe heavily; her grandson approaches her and gives her her heart medicine. He explains that talking about such a personal and stressful topic leaves his grandmother feeling tired and overwhelmed. She has a weak heart, "My days are getting shorter," she says. Aysha is an inspiration, throughout this interview she kept calm and never wavered or seemed weak. One would think she would be vulnerable to everything surrounding her, but on the contrary she was full of wisdom. When asked what she hoped for, she said with a confident tone, "My people will see better days than this; I know this for a fact. They will be happy again; mothers will no longer be forced to bury their children. The day of justice and freedom is near, I can feel it." As she said this, Aysha seemed certain that this war will not last very long. Many Palestinians have the same hopes as Aysha, they too are confident that the day will come when their people will be live in security again.

Aysha is one of many Palestinians who shares the same dream as millions, which is a liberated and a prosperous Palestine. As she stands up and leans on her cane she says, "We want our rights, we want justice, we want freedom on our land, and we want Palestine."

Aysha's final words were that she prays that once her soul rests, she hopes to be buried next to her husband's grave on the holy land of Palestine.

SAMPLE STUDENT ESSAY FOR PEER EDITING, RHETORICAL ANALYSIS
ASSIGNMENT

RHETORICAL ANALYSIS OF PRESIDENT REAGAN'S "CHALLENGER SPEECH"

FIVE, FOUR, THREE, TWO, ONE, WE HAVE LIFT OFF! THE SPACE SHUTTLE CHALLENGER HAS CLEARED THE LAUNCH PAD. This was supposed to be a glorious day in American history, a mile stone in the United States Space Program. Instead this day quickly turned into one of the most horrific scenes witnessed live by the American public, which included thousands of school children, who watched from the comfort and safety of their classrooms.

On January 28, 1986, the space shuttle Challenger was scheduled for launch in Florida. It would mark the second flight by the United States Space program and it was the first educational launch program. On this particular flight there was to be a teacher on board, she was the first teacher on a space shuttle as a result of a special program from NASA. Although there were some clear concerns regarding whether the shuttle should launch, NASA officials gave the green light and the mission moved forward. Within seconds of lift off, the space shuttle Challenger burst into flames and disintegrated in mid flight, instantly killing all seven passengers aboard. The nation was shocked, especially thousands of young children who eagerly watched the live coverage on television. Within hours of the explosion President Ronald Reagan went on live television and addressed the nation from the White House. President Reagan was scheduled to address the nation on that particular day to report on the state of the Union, instead he went on television and paid tribute to the Challenger Seven. President Reagan delivered one of the most inspirational, and motivational speeches of his tenure as the President of the United States. It is a speech, like all great speeches, that would out live his presidency, and be regarded as one of the great speeches of our time.

The nation stood still, not knowing what to make of the days events. In such times of sorrow people tend to need support, guidance, and reassurance. The American people needed someone to follow, a shoulder to lean on, a vision of the future, a leader. President Reagan went on live television and paid tribute to the "Challenger Seven" in a speech from the White House. President Reagan sat alone behind a large desk surrounded in the background by family pictures. President Reagan used his *ethos* as a credible individual; he was the leader of the free Nation. He gave the speech from the White House, which is clearly recognized by the American public as a symbol of power and security. The image of him sitting behind a great desk flanked by pictures of family and loved ones borrowing once again from their *ethos*. This was a not only the President of the United States delivering this speech, this was a husband, a father, and a son too.

The occasion for the speech was obvious: The Nation had just witnessed seven brave individuals perish before their very eyes. These brave souls were, husbands, sons, daughters, fathers, and they had paid the ultimate sacrifice for mankind. President Reagan portrayed all of these different roles played by each of the "Challenger Seven" from behind that desk. As the speech proceeded, President Reagan was careful to not down play the Challenger incident, but he appealed to *logos*, or logic, by saying "But we have never lost an astronaut in flight. We've never had a tragedy like this one." Here he used *pathos* to emphasize the severity of the incident while at the same time letting the nation know that there have been other brave astronauts who have also paid the ultimate price for the visions and progress of mankind. President Reagan throughout his speech used his words very carefully and with great insight. His words and the double meaning or relation to the events of the day made a huge impact on the delivery and acceptance of his speech by the American public. As he stated "Your loved ones were daring and brave, and they had that special grace, that spirit that says, Give me a challenge, and I'll meet it with joy." As one can see, President Reagan is using the word challenge here, this is a direct reference to the space shuttle Challenger.

President Reagan goes on to address the thousands of children who also witnessed the event, addressing the emotion or *pathos* of the occasion. He states, "And I want to say something to the schoolchildren of America who were watching the live coverage of the shuttle's take-off. I know it's hard to understand, but sometimes painful things like this happen. It's all part of the process of exploration and discovery. It is all part of taking a chance and expanding man's horizons. The future doesn't belong to the fainthearted; it belongs to the brave. The Challenger crew was pulling us into the future, and we'll continue to follow them." Here President Reagan's audience is the children, who in turn are the future of the nation. By saying that the Challenger was taking them towards the future, he is saying what everybody already knows. The children are the future of the nation and he is telling them that they must continue to move forward, for one day they will be the leaders of the country.

President Reagan's message is very clear: This was a tragedy, yet we as a nation must continue to move forward in order to honor the memory of the "Challenger Seven." President Reagan, utilizing *logos*, then mentions the NASA employees in his speech. Here he does not blame or degrade the space program or its employees. Instead he praises there hard work and dedication to the American people and the space program. He does not speculate on the cause of the explosion nor does he address any issues related to who is to blame. He completely omits any negative or accusatory comments in his speech. This was a very tactful and extremely intelligent move by Reagan. He knew the American public had many questions regarding the explosion. He also knew that those questions needed to be answered and that it was his responsibility to provide those answers to the nation. Yet on this day, and in this speech, it was not the right time to do so.

President Reagan in closing his speech borrows from the *ethos* of the past when he stated "There's a coincidence today. On this day three hundred and ninety years ago, the great explorer Sir Francis Drake died aboard ship off the coast of Panama… a historian later said, He lived by the sea, died on it, and was buried in it. Well, today, we can say of the Challenger crew: their dedication was, like Drake's complete."

President Reagan's speech on the space shuttle Challenger served several purposes. First, it paid tribute to the seven astronauts who lost their lives in the explosion. Second, it provided the nation with a much needed reassurance that everything was going to be all right. And although this was terrible accident and set back for our country, he also left no doubt that the Nations commitment to NASA and the space program would not only survive, but continue to advance forward into the future.

SAMPLE STUDENT ESSAY FOR PEER EDITING, RESEARCH PAPER ASSIGNMENT

> *This student research paper argues that marketing through blogging is not an effective technique for corporations. Notice the somewhat unusual narrative introduction and conclusion.*
>
> ## MARKETING THROUGH BLOGGING: GOOD STRATEGY?
>
> The personnel department at J&M Incorporated [a fictional multinational corporation] sent Alice Miller [also a fictitious name] to see the director of the marketing division for potential hiring because of her experience in using blogging for marketing products. During her interview, the marketing team director said, "Explain to me this revolutionary idea you have in your application—'Marketing through blogging'? Why would we want to use this strategy to market our products?"
>
> Without hesitation, Alice began her explanation. "First and foremost, blogging is a form of communication on the Internet. It is very much like a diary or newsletter written in a very easygoing language that everyone can comprehend. This medium of information exchange has become extremely popular among the younger generations as well as fairly popular among older generations. We could use this form of communication to market J&M Inc. products in a word of mouth form. Creating a blog for J&M Inc. to market the products would bring the company down to the consumer level, allowing the consumers to feel like the J&M Inc. is just like one of them — not the overwhelming powerhouse it is."
>
> The term "blog" was coined by Jorn Barger in 1999. Barger defined a Weblog as "a webpage where a weblogger (sometimes called a blogger, or a pre-surfer) 'logs' all of the other webpages she finds interesting" (qtd. in Goodwin par. 3). Blogs have since then evolved into a myriad of other things. Kathleen Goodwin of ClickZ Network: Solutions for Marketers gives today's definition of blogs as "a Web page that serves as a publicly-accessi-

ble personal journal for an individual. Typically updated daily, blogs often reflect the personality of the author" (par. 3). General bloggers believe that "a blog is often a mixture of what is happening in a person's life and what is happening on the web, a kind of hybrid diary/guide site" ("Blog" par. 1). There are many different types of blogs. There are personal blogs, political blogs, cooking blogs and cat owner blogs; the list goes on and on. There are as many types of blogs as there are different things in the world. One genre of blogs is called "Businessblogs," or "b-blogs," a term originated by Goodwin (par. 6). B-blogs were created when marketers for different companies saw the potential of the word-of-mouth advertising. Goodwin stated that b-blogs

> offer organizations a platform where information, data, and opinion can be shared and traded among employees, customers, partners, and prospects in a way previously impossible: a two-way, open exchange. Companies can (and should) encourage self-publishing from all corners of the organization. (Goodwin par. 7)

However, not all companies present their blogs as b-blogs. There are b-blogs that serve as communications within the same company, with their competitors and with their customers. Those fit nicely into the definition of a blog. Unfortunately, there are some companies creating b-blogs that do not seem to comprehend that blogs are meant to be a bottom-up type of communication, not a top-down way of communication. These blogs are written by paid professionals posing as consumers. Blogs are supposed to start with the consumer and flow upward to the companies in a type of feedback form. Companies that are trying to market a product by way of posing as consumers when they write their blogs are ignoring the form of true blogging. They want the information they are paying to produce and spread to have the feel of a blog – honest and person-to-person style. However, it is impossible to produce a blog with genuine qualities due to the undeniable fact that it is a company talking to a person, not a person talking to another person. Wade Roush, author of "Your Ad Here," gave an example of how a company attempted to create a blog and make it appear as if it truly came from the consumer level. He cited this as being the origin of the controversy of whether blogs ought to be used for advertising. Roush says it all began in December of 2004 when a company called Marqui in Portland, Oregon, offered to pay 20 writers to blog about its software (21). After the term was up, the bloggers paid by Marqui had the same sentiment – being paid to blog was just not the same as blogging of their own free will, and there was no evidence that the blogging marketing campaign did anything to help Marqui gain anything other than controversy in the media (22).

Some bloggers, and blog readers find that the idea of paying bloggers to write about products or insert ads destroy the art of blogging as the public knows it. Because it destroys the concept of blogging as most have come to understand it, marketing through blogging is a terrible strategy. If the medium is destroyed and transformed into something else completely in the public's eye, then there will be no more advertising through blogging as blogging itself will not exist in the same light. The demise of advertising through blogging is inevitable in that by doing it, the medium is destroyed.

Blogs are transformed into something else through commercialization. Matt Haughey, who has done work for Metafilter, a search engine company, believed that commercializing blogs taint the medium by "writing entries to please your readers and advertisers, not yourself, posting entries because you have to, to get paid, lazy fact-checking to push things in under deadlines, conflicts of interest, and lack of disclosure of who is paying you and why" (qtd. in Copeland par. 37). Haughey pointed out several known issues with making blogs commercial. He argues that using blogs in a commercial setting would not be a good strategy for several reasons: the inevitable factual inaccuracies, bias, and lack of disclosure. Molly Holzschlag, a blogger at www.molly.com, stated, "I could not tolerate the feeling of having to post my blog based on a contractual obligation. I realized my blog is something I want to be more spontaneous with; it's the only way I can write to it properly" (qtd. in Roush 22). Holzschlag wanted to remain true to one of the basic foundations of blogging: spontaneity. Blogs cannot be planned out and feel genuine.

Holzschlag is not alone in her sentiment that being required to blog about a product is not what blogging is all about. Bloggers believe that blogging is a place to be spontaneous, opinionated and honest — not a place to be forced to write any specific thing. One blogger named Jason Calacanis argued, "To take money to blog about something—and disclose it or not—works against the public's expectation that blogs are, first and foremost, upfront and honest" (qtd. in Roush 22).

One prime example, widely known in the blogging community, of a b-blog failing horribly due to the conflict with the meaning of blogging is that of the "Vichy" blog created by a division of L'Oreal by the name of Vichy. The blog was supposed to promote an anti-aging cream. The paid writers for the blog posed as a woman named Claire who was constantly complaining about not getting enough sleep and not having enough energy to party. The pictures they posted of Claire were of a flawless model, gazing into a mirror. Not many people could relate, much less believe, the story of Claire. Shel Israel and Robert Scoble, authors of *Naked Controversies* wrote,

> It took only a few hours for the blogosphere to react strongly to the negative. Comments began pouring in, declaring that this was not a blog, that the site had severely limited blog features, that people did not believe Claire was a real person and that Vichy was foisting a fraud on the public. (par. 7)

Obviously, character blogs created by companies to pose as a common consumer cannot work as the everyday person sees right through them due to their conflicting definition of a true blog.

The second biggest argument against the marketing through blogging strategy lies within the accuracy of the material presented within the b-blogs. As the majority of blogs on the Internet are written at the blogger's leisure, extremely small amounts of blogs are actually reviewed before being posted to the web. Catherine Seipp echoed the problem of accuracy in blogs in one of her articles when she quoted *The American Prospect's* Natasha Berger as being "worried about 'the serious problem of quality control in the increasingly powerful blogging world,' which she also complained is 'editor-free,'" (Seipp par. 4). Seipp went on to provide information that "*The American Prospect* and *The Nation* seem to imagine that blogs, which are by definition creatures of the free market, ought to be pre-approved by some sort of official bureaucracy" (par. 4). The argument against marketing through blogging due to factual inaccuracies stems back to the definition that blogs typically are written by everyday people and not scholars or experts. Eric Alterman of the Neiman Reports on Harvard.edu writes: "Because blogging requires no credentials whatever – not even the judgment of an editor or personnel resources person – absolutely anybody with access to a computer can do it....[it is] swirling around out there, unedited, unchecked and largely untrue" (Alterman 87). There is no way to get the entire blogosphere, or even a small fraction of it, to begin having their blogs reviewed and checked for factual inaccuracies. Because of this, the medium will continue to be viewed suspiciously by blog readers.

Corporate bloggers ought to have their posts reviewed before posting as there may be legal ramifications if inaccurate information is allowed to be posted. However, in order to keep up with those blog readers that respond to posts and ask questions or leave comments that require addressing, the corporate blogger posts will not have the time to be reviewed. The responses and new posts will have to be posted in real time in response to the consumers' inquiries in order to be taken seriously.

Robert Scobleizer wrote in his article, "The Corporate Weblog Manifesto" many different suggestions and warnings to those venturing into corporate blogging. He acknowledged that if posting on a corporate weblog, there will be factual inaccuracies and gave the advice to corporate bloggers to correct themselves as soon as possible (Scobleizer par. 9). He warns about the possibility of having to post things that may not be legally correct. "If it takes you two weeks to answer what's going on in the marketplace because you're scared of what your legal hit will be, then …[y]our competitors will figure it out and outmaneuver you" (par. 18). By this, Scobleizer means to say that by blogging factual inaccuracies, the readers will figure it out – whether they are the company's competitors or the consumers. Once the readers figure it out, the company loses credibility. Scobleizer gives the advice to react quickly – though regardless of how quickly the corporate blogger attempts to correct posts that would have been caught by an editor in the first place – the public has still seen the mistake.

Returning to Alice Miller's interview, the director of the marketing program told her, "After careful consideration of your application, we have found your ideas to be incompatible with the marketing mission of J&M Inc. We will not be hiring you. We thank you for taking the time to come here and share with us today." With that, Alice smiled politely and went through the motions of a formal polite goodbye. She did not yet understand what the marketing director knew--that marketing through blogging is not a good strategy primarily because it is misleading, ineffective, and fraught with possibility of error.

Works Cited

Alterman, Eric. "Determining the Value of Blogs." *Neiman Reports.*
Harvard U. Fall 2003. Web. 15 Sept. 2008.

"Blog." *MarketingTerms.com: Internet Marketing Reference.* Web. 4 Oct.
2008.

Copeland, Henry. "Blogonomics: Making a Living from Blogging." *Press
flex.* Pressflex: The Webmaster for Publishers. 28 May 2002. Web. 4
Oct. 2005.

Goodwin, Kathleen. "Meet the B-Blog." *ClickZ Experts.* Web. 4 Oct. 2008.

Israel, Shel and Robert Scoble. "Chapter 10: Doing it Wrong." *Naked
Controversies.* 14 July 2005. Web. 19 Oct. 2008.

Roush, Wade. "Your Ad Here." *Technology Review.* July 2005:
21-22. Massachusetts Institute of Technology. Web. 26 Sept. 2008.

Scobleizer, Robert. "The Corporate Weblog Manifesto." *Scobleizer
Microsoft Geek Blogger.* 26. Feb. 2003. Web. 1 Nov. 2008.

Seipp, Catherine. "Online Uprising." *American Journalism Review.* June
2002. Web. 4 Oct. 2008.

Avoid Plagiarism

Plagiarism is defined by the Writing Program Administrators (WPA), a group of English professors who direct college composition programs: "In an instructional setting, plagiarism occurs when a writer deliberately uses someone else's language, ideas, or other original (not common-knowledge) material without acknowledging its source." A keyword here is "deliberately." Instructors, however, may have difficulty distinguishing between accidental and deliberate plagiarism. The burden is upon you as the writer to give credit where credit is due. These are some examples of plagiarism:

- Turning in a paper that was written by someone else as your own. This includes obtaining a paper from an Internet term paper mill.
- Copying a paper or any part of a paper from a source without acknowledging the source in the proper format.
- Paraphrasing materials from a source without documentation.
- Copying materials from a text but treating it as your own, leaving out quotation marks and acknowledgement.

Choosing When to Give Credit

Need to Document	No Need to Document
• When you are using or referring to somebody else's words or ideas from a magazine, book, newspaper, song, TV program, movie, Web page, computer program, letter, advertisement, or any other medium. • When you use information gained through interviewing another person. • When you copy the exact words or a "**unique phrase**" from somewhere. • When you reprint any diagrams, illustrations, charts, and pictures. • When you use ideas that others have given you in conversation or over email.	• When you are writing your own experiences, your own observations, your own insights, your own thoughts, your own conclusions about a subject. • When you are using "**common knowledge**" — folklore, common sense observations, shared information within your field of study or cultural group. • When you are compiling generally accepted facts. • When you are writing up your own experimental results.

The Online Writing Lab (OWL) at Purdue University provides an excellent handout on avoiding plagiarism, including this box about when to give credit to sources. See http://owl.english. purdue.edu.

When is it necessary to cite a source? If you are writing that the Space Shuttle Columbia disaster happened in 2003, do you need to cite your source? No, because you could find that information in any of a number of places. What if you use information from a *New York Times* article about how U.S. fast food eating habits are spreading to Europe? Yes, if you are going to paraphrase or quote from the article. The table above, from the Purdue University Online Writing Lab, gives more examples of when to cite sources.

DOCUMENTING SOURCES

Academic writing mandates students document their sources. Documenting sources allows the reader to evaluate the writer's research in regard to value and credibility. Several styles of documentation are widely acceptable in the university, to include MLA (Modern Language Association), APA (American Psychological Association), CBE (Council of Biology Editors), also called Scientific Style, and CMS (Chicago Manual of Style). This book focuses on MLA and APA styles. Each style of documentation offers both parenthetical (in-text) documentation and bibliographical documentation. In other words, every source must be cited within the text and at the end of the work. Recent technological advances have opened a wealth of electronic databases and independent websites offering instant access to valuable sources.

Students should not feel it is necessary to memorize documentation citation formats. They can always refer to the official handbooks for MLA, APA, CBE, and Chicago documentation styles. The Purdue University Online Writing Lab (OWL) offers an excellent summary of the different documentation styles and links to resources for each. Go to the home page, http://owl.english.purdue. edu and select "Handouts and Materials," then "Research and Documenting Sources," that will lead you to an abundance of useful handouts. Practice in proper documentation will ensure a better understanding of academic writing, familiarity with sources, and the ethical responsibility of crediting original authors.

Challenges in Documenting Electronic Publications

Changeable Nature of Electronic Sources

Although many documents posted on the Internet share characteristics of print documents such as title, author, and publication information, in other ways they are like television programs or live performances because the reader looking for cited documents cannot depend that the copy of cited information they locate on the Internet will be the same as the one the author accessed. Electronic publications can be easily updated or changed and may be removed from public access without notice. Thus, date of access (or retrieval) becomes important because it may provide information about a version of a text or the existence of a text that has since been removed from public access.

In the past, MLA Style recommended including the URL (web address) of documents in the Works Cited list. However, more recently MLA has taken the position that including that information has limited value because they are prone to change and are cumbersome in any case. Current recommendations are that students include URLs only when the material would otherwise be difficult to locate or if the instructor requires it. If you do include a URL, enclose them in angle brackets and follow with a period. For example, the website for the New York Times would be <http://www.nytimes.com>.

APA Style suggests including the elements of a citation in the same order, as you would for a print source, adding information about electronic retrieval after the standard information. However, APA also recognizes that information such as author, publication date, publisher, or even title may be missing in an electronic source. APA suggests giving the DOI (Digital Object Identifier), a unique alphanumeric string that is a persistent link, whenever possible. If it is not available, APA recommends giving the URL of the item being cited.

Citing Page Numbers

Many documents on the Internet do not give information generally available for print publications such as author, page number, or publisher. Students should provide whatever such information is available. For example, when retrieving an item from an electronic database or website, students are often given a choice of opening either an HTML (webpage) document or a PDF (Adobe Portable Document Format) document. If a PDF version is given, students should select it, as it is a representation of the original source and has page numbers which can be cited. Since many articles are not offered in the PDF format, however, students, when utilizing other file formats, cannot cite actual page numbers. In the case of full text HTML documents, you should cite section titles and paragraph numbers when they are available. If section and/or paragraph numbers are not available, you cannot cite them.

MLA STYLE

For MLA style, also refer to the *MLA Handbook for Writers of Research Papers* and the MLA Web site, http://www.mla.org.

BIBLIOGRAPHICAL DOCUMENTATION

In MLA Style, this is called either the Works Cited page or an Annotated Bibliography. The title, Works Cited or Annotated Bibliography, should appear centered on the top margin of the last page of a researched essay. The Works Cited page should be double-spaced with no extra line spacing between entries. The first line of each entry begins at the margin, and all subsequent lines of a particular entry are indented 5 spaces on the left margin. All entries should be in alphabetical order. The Annotated Bibliography is formatted like the Works Cited page with the addition of an annotation or description of the source in a paragraph following the citation. The following entries are typical citations for an MLA style. Examples are offered for both print, online, and database versions, when applicable.

Two or More Selections from the Same Print Collection or Anthology

> **Note**: To avoid repetition on the list of works cited, cite the anthology or reader as a separate entry. Then cross-reference entries to the anthology as in the example below.

Burns, Gary. "Marilyn Manson and the Apt Pupils of Littleton." Petracca and Sorapure 284-90. Print.

Fox, Roy. "Salespeak." Petracca and Sorapure 56-72.

Petracca, Michael and Madeleine Sorapure, eds. *Common Culture: Reading and Writing About American Popular Culture*. 5th ed. Upper Saddle River: Pearson, 2007. Print.

Note: Alphabetize each entry among other entries on the works cited page. Do not group the entries from the anthology together unless they fall next to one another alphabetically. Also, remember that you will have no parenthetical citation referencing the editors Petracca and Sorapure. You should cite Burns and Fox in the parenthetical citations in your paper.

Book or Novel

Nicolson, Adam. *Seize the Fire: Heroism, Duty, and the Battle of Trafalgar*. New York: HarperCollins, 2005. Print.

Book with Multiple Editors

Mennuti, Rosemary B., Arthur Freeman, and Ray W. Christner, eds. *Cognitive-Behavioral Interventions: A Handbook for Practice*. New York: Routledge, 2006. Print.

Online Edition of Book or Novel

James, Henry. *The American*. 1877. Fiction: *The Eserver Collection*. Web. 15 June 2008.

(This book was published before 1900, so the name and city of the publisher are not needed. For more recent books, give the print information first, then the information about web publication.)

Scholarly Article with Continuous Pagination

Andrews, Howard. "Writing and the Internet." *Teaching English in the Two Year College 21* (1999): 233-51. Print.

Book Review

Schneider, Robert J. Rev. of *Modern Physics and Ancient Faith*, by Stephen M. Barr. *Anglican Theological Review 86* (2004): 506-07. Print.

An Editorial

Wolfe, Gregory. "Emerson vs. Hawthorne." Editorial. *Image: A Journal of the Arts and Religion 12* (1995-96): 3-4. Print.

Scholarly Article Online

Kimihiko, Yoshii and Tonogai Yasuhide. "Water Content Using Karl-Fisher Aquametry and Loss on Drying Determinations Using Thermogravi meter for Pesticide Standard Materials." *Journal of Health Science 50. 2* (2004): 142-47. Web. 2 Jun. 2005.

Note: This entry is for an article in a journal with text available online. The print information, such as the volume number, is given first. Then the word "Web" indicates that it is also available on the Internet. If the journal is online only, it may not give page numbers. In that case, substitute "n. page" for the page numbers.

Scholarly Article from Online Database

McMichael, Anthony J. "Population, Environment, Disease, and Survival: Past Patterns, Uncertain Futures." 145-48. Lexis-Nexis. Web. 22 May 2006.

Note: The name of the database is given after the publication information, and it is followed by the word "Web" and the date the article was accessed.

An Entire Website

Science Daily. Eds. Dan Hogan and Michele Hogan. Web. 2007. 19 Oct. 2008. <http://sciencedaily.com>.

(MLA allows you to give the URL of the website if you need to do so for clarification. If you include the URL, place it in brackets.)

Article from a Magazine

Deboer, Peter. "Junior Achievers." *Sports Illustrated* 6 Jun. 2005: 17-18. Print.

Article from an Online Magazine

Winant, Gabriel. "Who Hates Who in Iran." *Salon.* Salon Media Group, 19 June 2009. Web. 20 June 2009.

Note: The title of the magazine is followed by the publisher or sponsor of the site, a comma, and the date of the publication. MLA uses this format because it does not consider online-only magazines to be periodicals.

Magazine Article from an Online Database

Seltzer, Larry. "Tales of a Professional Social Engineer." *PC Magazine* 7 Jun.
2005: 105-111. Academic Search Premier. Web. 22 Apr. 2005.

(Give the print information first, then the name of the database, the
word "Web," and the date accessed.)

Newspaper Article Online

Pear, Robert. "States Intervene After Drug Plans Hit Early Snags." *New York
Times*. New York Times Co., 7 Jan. 2006. Web. 15 Feb. 2006.

(MLA considers websites for newspapers to be non-periodical, so the
format follows the title of the newspaper with the name of the publisher of the website, a comma, and the date of publication for the
article, the word "Web," and the date accessed.)

Newspaper Article from Online Database

Kolata, Gina. "Koreans Report Ease in Cloning for Stem Cells." *New York
Times* 20 May 2005: A1+. Academic Search Premier. Web. 8 May
2008.

(Give the print information first, then the name of the database, the
word "Web," and the date accessed. In this case, the plus sign indicates
that the pagination is not continuous.)

Government Document

"El Chamizal Dispute: Compliance with Convention of the Chamizal." 1964.
US Senate Hearing. Cleofas Calleros Papers. University of Texas at El
Paso Library Special Collections. 33-9. Print.

Government Document Online

Travis, William Barret. "Letter from the Alamo, 1836." Texas State Library &
Archives Commission. Web. 15 Apr. 2005.

Government Document from Online Database

"United Nations Resolutions on Operation Desert Storm." Aug-Nov 1990.
Essential Documents in American History: 1492-Present. 1-17
Academic Search Premier. Web. 8 May 2008.

Educational Website (they usually end in edu)

Turner, Logan. "Texas Farming: Life of a Migratory Wheat Cutter." Interview with Jack Waldroop. Texas Farming Oral History Files. 2004. Web. 15 Apr. 2005.

An Advertisement

The Fitness Fragrance by Ralph Lauren. Advertisement. GQ Apr. 1997: 111-12. Print.

A Television Program

"Circle of Life." By Alton Brown. Dir. Alton Brown. *Good Eats*. Food Network. 13 Oct. 2007. Television.

A Film on DVD

The Lord of the Rings: The Return of the King. Dir. Peter Jackson. New Line, 2003. DVD-ROM.

An Interview

Blackmun, Harry. Interview with Ted Koppel and Nina Totenberg. *Nightline*. ABC. WABC, New York. 5 Apr. 1994. Television.

Doe, Jane. Personal interview. 18 Oct. 2007.

MLA Parenthetical or (In-text) Documentation

Parenthetical documentation refers to the process of citing sources within the text. Citing sources within the text is necessary for students to indicate when they are using the words, thoughts, or ideas that are not their own and borrowed from an outside source. Whether students use a direct quote, a paraphrase or summary of the information, they must properly provide credit to the original author(s) of that source. Using appropriate sources for support and documenting these sources accurately adds to the credibility and value of a student's essay. The following examples provide a guideline to proper parenthetical documentation.

Direct Quote (three lines or less)

"Scientists estimate that the rangewide population of the San Joaquin kit fox prior to 1930 was 8,000..." (Conover 44).

Direct Quote (more than three lines) (Indent 10 spaces and block.)

Conover's 2001 study of the San Joaquin kit fox found the following:

> For the most part, in the "real" world, kit foxes escape their predators and the high temperatures of their desert environment by spending the day underground in a den. In Bakersfield, they follow suite. Kit foxes move every couple of weeks to a new den. Moving to different dens may be one reason why they have persisted; the constantly changing abodes provided new places to hide. (199)

Direct Quote when the author is named in the text

Hildebrand states that "generals of Alexander the Great brought news to Europe of vegetable wool which grew in tufts of trees in India" (144).

Information from printed source, but it is not a direct quote

It is common to see an Osprey make its nest on an electric power pole (Askew 34).

Electronic Sources

Many electronic sources are not numbered with pages unless it is a PDF file. If paragraphs are numbered, use numbers following the abbreviation, par. Most often the source will not have page, paragraph, section or screen numbers. In this case, include no numbers in the parentheses.
(Bussell par. 3)

APA Style

For APA style, also refer to the *Publication Manual of the American Psychological Association* and the website provided by the American Psychological Association, http://www.apastyle.org, which offers free tutorials for APA style.

Bibliographical Documentation

In APA Style, this is called either the References or Annotated Bibliography. The title, References or Annotated Bibliography, should appear centered on the top margin of the last page of a researched essay. The

References or Annotated Bibliography page should be double-spaced with no extra line spacing between entries. The first line of each entry begins at the margin, and all subsequent lines of a particular entry are indented on the left margin 5 spaces for a References Page and 7 for an Annotated Bibliography. All entries should be in alphabetical order. The Annotated Bibliography is formatted like the References page with the addition of an annotation or description of the source in a paragraph following the citation.

> **Note:** APA suggests that when you are citing a source from the web or an online database you should give the DOI (Digital Object Identifier) of the source in the References List. If the DOI is not available, you can give the URL (web address) for the text. APA does not require that you give the date you access a source on the Internet unless you have reason to believe that the text may change or disappear from the Internet. Also note that if you cite an entire website, simply include the website address in parentheses in the text with no entry in the References page. The following entries are typical citations for APA style. Examples are offered for both print, online, and database versions, when applicable.

Book or Novel

Nicolson, A. (2005). *Seize the fire: Heroism, duty, and the battle of Trafalgar.* New York: HarperCollins.

Book or Novel with Multiple Editors

Mennuti, R.B., Freeman, A., and Christner, R.W. (Eds.). (2006). *Cognitive-behavioral interventions in educational settings: A handbook for practice.* New York: Routledge.

Book or Novel Online Edition

James, H.(1960). The American. Retrieved from http://eserver.org/fiction/novel.html
(If the book has a DOI, then give that instead of the URL).

Book Review

Schneider, R. J. (2004). [Review of the book *Modern physics and ancient faith*]. *Anglican Theological Review, 86*, 506-07.

Scholarly Article

Andrews, H. (1992). Writing and the Internet. *Teaching English in the Two-Year College, 21*, 233-251.

Scholarly Article Online with a DOI

Kubzansky, L. D. and Martin, L. T. (2009) Early manifestations of personality and adult health: a life course perspective. Health Psychology 38.3, 364-372. DOI: 10.1037/a0014428

Scholarly Article Online without a DOI

Kimihiko, Y., & Yasuhide, T. (2004). Water content using Karl-Fisher aqua metry and loss on drying determinations using thermogravimeter for pesticide standard materials. Journal of Health Science, 50, 142-147. Retrieved from http://www. jstage.jst.go.jp/browse/jhs/50/2/_contents

Article from a Magazine

Deboer, P. (2005, June). Junior achievers. *Sports Illustrated*, pp. 17-18.

Article from a Magazine Online

Banks, S. (2005, April). Hill country. *Texas Monthly Online*. Retrieved from http://www.texasmonthly.com/previous/2005-04-01/feature3

Newspaper Article

Trembacki, P.(2000, December 5). Brees hopes to win Heisman for team. *The Dallas Morning News,* p. 20.

Newspaper Article Online

Aguilar, M.(2005, March 28). Miners anxious to get back to work. The El Paso Times. Retrieved from http:www.elpasotimesonline/03/28/05.htm

Government Document

El Chamizal dispute: Compliance with convention of the Chamizal. (1964). *US Senate Hearing*. Cleofas Calleros Papers. University of Texas at El Paso Library Special Collections (#33-9).

Government Document Online

Travis, W. B. (2005). Letter from the Alamo, 1836. Retrieved from Texas State Library & Archives Commission, http//www.tslstate.tx.us/treasures/republic/Alamo/travis01.gov

A Film or DVD

Coen, E. & Coen, J. (Producers and directors). (2007). *No country for old men* [Motion picture]. United States: Paramount Vantage.

A Television Program

Martin, D. (Reporter). (2008, March 2). The Pentagon's ray gun (television series episode). In M. Walsh (Producer), *60 Minutes*. New York: CBS News.

APA Parenthetical or (In-text) Documentation

Direct Quote (three lines or less)
"Scientists estimate that the rangewide population of the San Joaquin kit fox prior to 1930 was 8,000..." (Conover, 2001, p. 44).

Direct Quote (more than three lines) (Indent 5 spaces and block.)
Conover's 2001 study of the San Joaquin kit fox found the following:

> For the most part, in the "real" world kit foxes escape their predators and the high temperatures of their desert environment by spending the day underground in a den. In Bakersfield, they follow suite. Kit foxes move every couple of weeks to a new den. Moving to different dens may be one reason why they have persisted; the constantly changing abodes provided new places to hide. (p. 199)

Direct Quote when the author is named in the text

Hildebrand (2004) stated that "generals of Alexander the Great brought news to Europe of vegetable wool which grew in tufts of trees in India" (p. 144).

Information from printed source, but it is not a direct quote

It is common to see an Osprey make its nest on an electric power pole (Askew, year, p. 34).

Naming the author of a reference in your text, but not using a direct quote

Thompson (2002) maintained that...

In 2002, Thompson discovered...

Electronic Sources (Again, many electronic sources are not numbered with pages. If your source provides section notations or paragraph number, indicate those. Use the paragraph ¶ symbol or the abbreviation para. and number.)

(Bussell, 2000, ¶ 9)

(Morrison, 2001, Introductory section, para. 2)

CITATIONS

"20 Years Later, San Ysidro McDonald's Massacre Remembered." North County Times. 17 July 2004. <http://www.nctimes.com/articles/2004/07/18/news/top_stories/16_42_237_17_04.txt>.

"500 Years of Chicana Women's History." Facebook. <http://www.facebook.com/group.php?gid=13082534326>. 9 June 2009.

Academic Search Complete. EBSCO. <http://www.ebscohost.com>. 9 June 2009.

Adams, Scott. "Dilbert." Comic Strip. Dist. By United Feature Syndicate

Ann Nixon Cooper. <http://www.annnixoncooper.com/>. 9 June 2009.

BMW Advertisement <http://www.coloribus.com/adsarchive/prints/used-cars-you-know-youre-not-the-first-202953/>. 9 June 2009.

Calder Hall Nuclear Power Plant. Photograph. "Nuclear Power." Wikipedia. <http://en.wikipedia.org/wiki/Nuclear_power>.

"Choosing When to Give Credit." The Purdue Online Writing Lab. <http://owl.english.purdue.edu/owl/printable/589/>. 9 June 2009.

Cohen, Leonard & Sharon Robinson. "Everybody Knows." *Columbia Records*. February 1988. LP/digital recording.

Cook, Mariana "A Couple in Chicago." The New Yorker. 19 January 2009. <http://www.newyorker.com/reporting/2009/01/19/090119fa_fact_cook>.

Davis, Lisa Selin. "Does Facebook Replace Face Time or Enhance It?" Time. 18 January 2009. <http://www.time.com/time/nation/article/0,8599,1871627,00.html>.

"I'm a Mac." Apple Advertisement. CNET. 20 March 20008. <http://news.cnet.com/8301-13860_3-9898440-56.html>.

Infomine. < http://infomine.ucr.edu/>. 9 June 2009.

"Jet Blue Airways' Customer Bill of Rights." JetBlue Airways. July 2008. <www.jetblue.com/p/about/ourcompany/promise/Bill_Of_Rights.pdf>.

Judson, Olivia. "Let's Get Rid of Darwinism." The New York Times. 15 July 2008. <http://judson.blogs.nytimes.com/2008/07/15/lets-get-rid-of-darwinism>.

King, Jr., Dr. Martin Luther. "I Have a Dream." <http://www.americanrhetoric.com/speeches/mlkihaveadream.htm>.

Lucas, Stephen E. "The Stylistic Artistry of the Declaration of Independence." The National Archives. 1989. <http://www.archives.gov/exhibits/charters/declaration_style.html>.

Obama, Barack. "President-Elect Victory Speech." American Rhetoric. <http://www.americanrhetoric.com/speeches/convention2008/barackobamavictoryspeech.htm>.

Schwartz, Peter and Spencer Reiss. "How Clean, Green Atomic Energy Can Stop Global Warming." Wired. February 2005. <http://www.wired.com/wired/archive/13.02/nuclear.html>.

Scott, Stanley S. "Smokers Get a Raw Deal." New York Times. 29 December 1984. http://legacy.library.ucsf.edu/tid/fkn85e00

Skinner, E. Benjamin. "People for Sale." Foreign Policy. March-April 2008.

Toyota Advertisement<http://bp0.blogger.com/_c4ReDuPmgq0/RzPGN7vwibI/AAAAAAAAAGg/uj2DJHVdXXo/s1600-h/toyota-zero-emissions.jpg>. 9 June 2009.

Turk, Carolyn. "A Woman Can Learn Anything a Man Can." Newsweek. 5 April 2004: 12.

Williams, Terri. "Hospital Tramples Smokers' Rights with Total Ban." The Palm Beach Post. 14 July 2008. <http://www.palmbeachpost.com/opinion/content/opinion/epaper/2008/07/24/thursdaywebletters_0724.html.>

Wright, Don. "Obama Grammarian Cartoon." International Herald Tribune. 20 January 2009. <http://www.gocomics.com/features/224/feature_items/406768?msg_id=261940,406768>.

Index

Praxis Alphabetical Index

NOTES

NOTES

NOTES

NOTES

NOTES

NOTES